Cozy Cats

Family Coloring Book

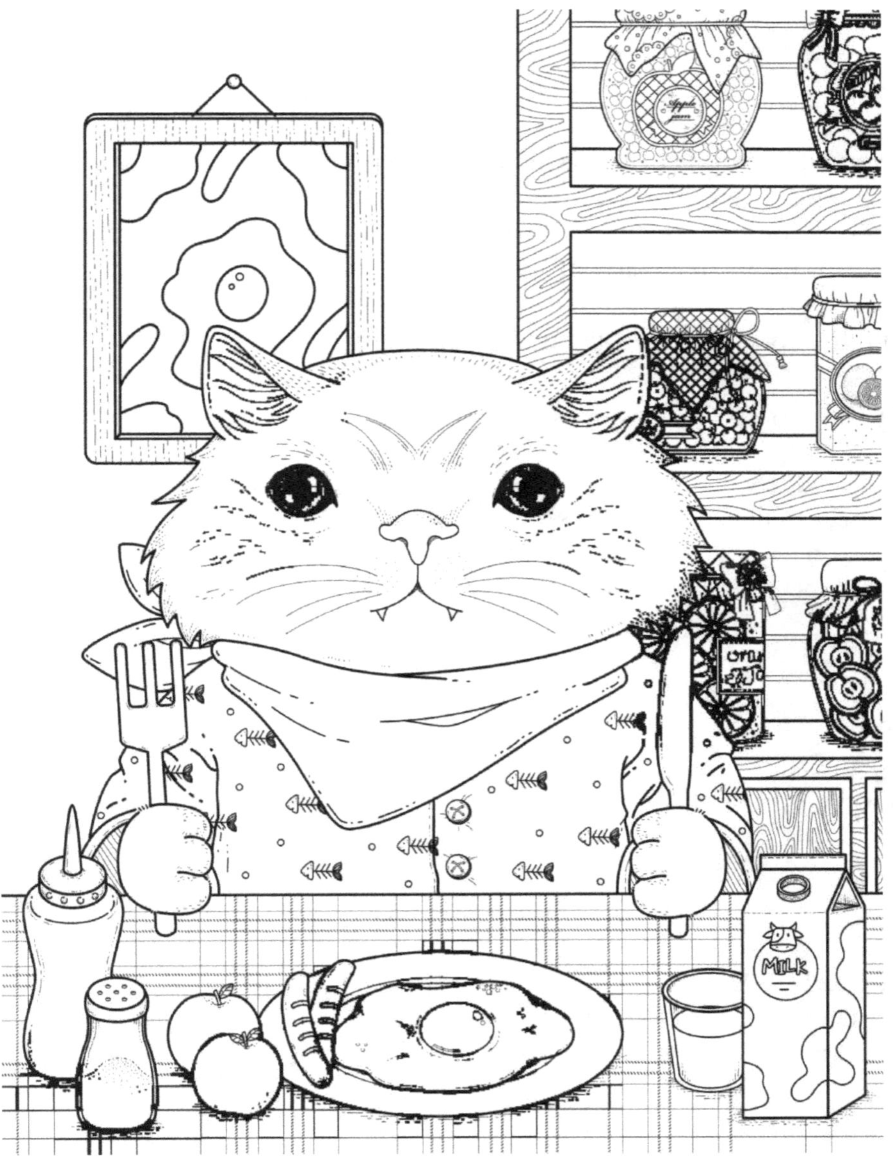

Patricia Rockwell

Cozy Cat Press

Dedicated to Cozette, the Cozy Cat Press mascot

For information, email Cozy Cat Press, cozycatpress@gmail.com or visit our website at: www.cozycatpress.com

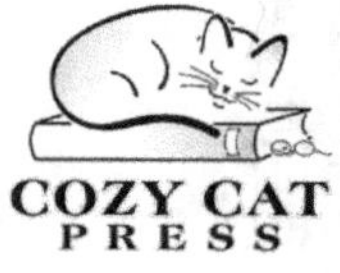

ISBN: 978-1-952579-03-5
Printed in the United States of America

10 9 8 7 6 5 4 3 2 1

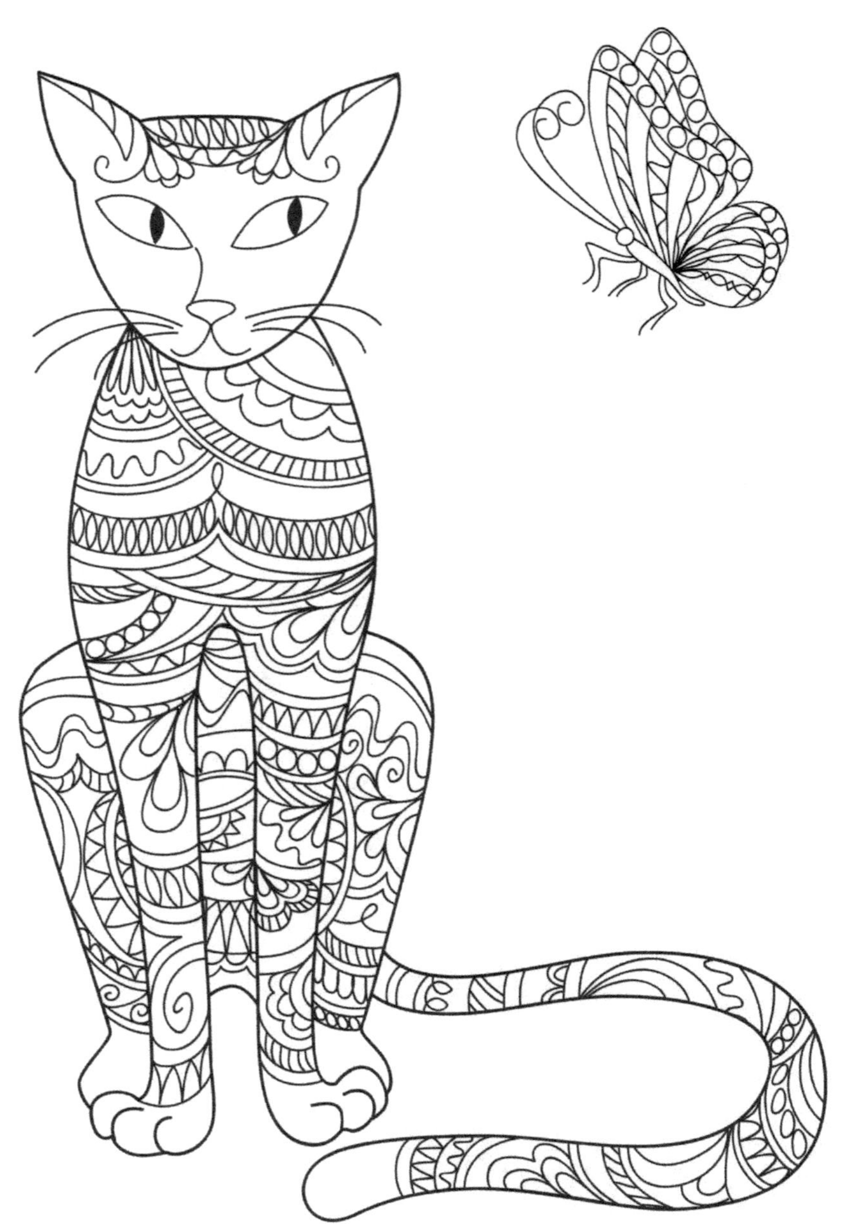

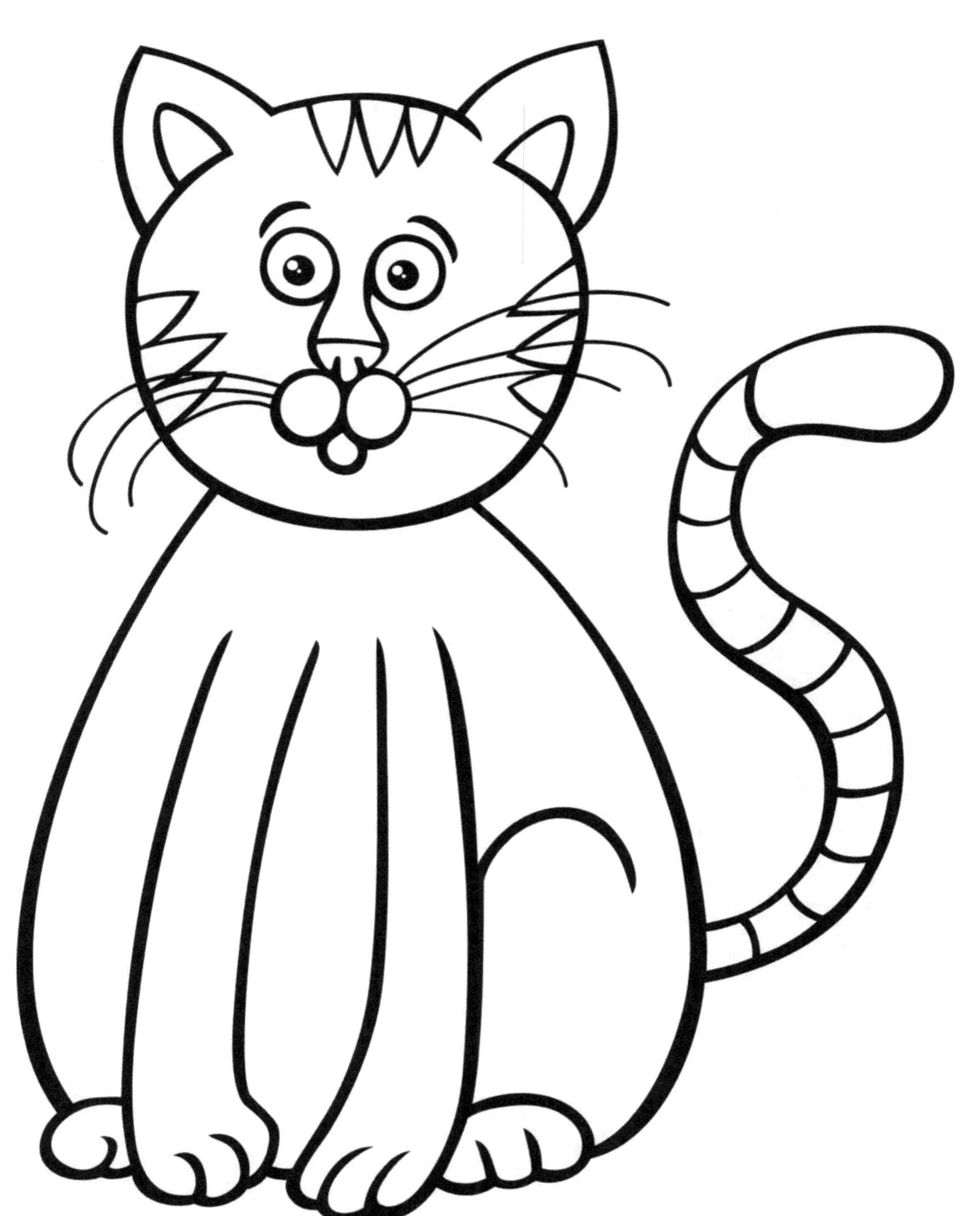

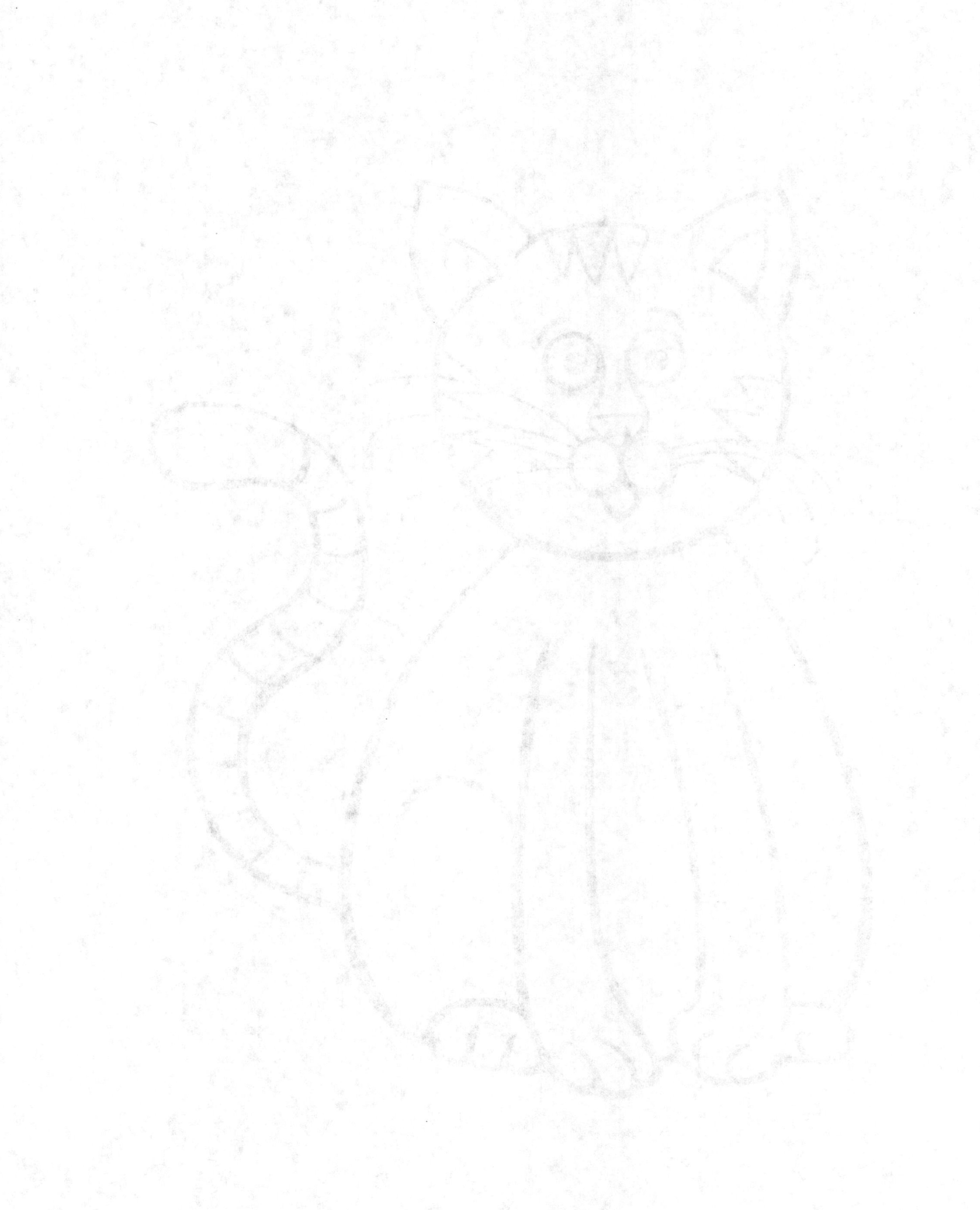

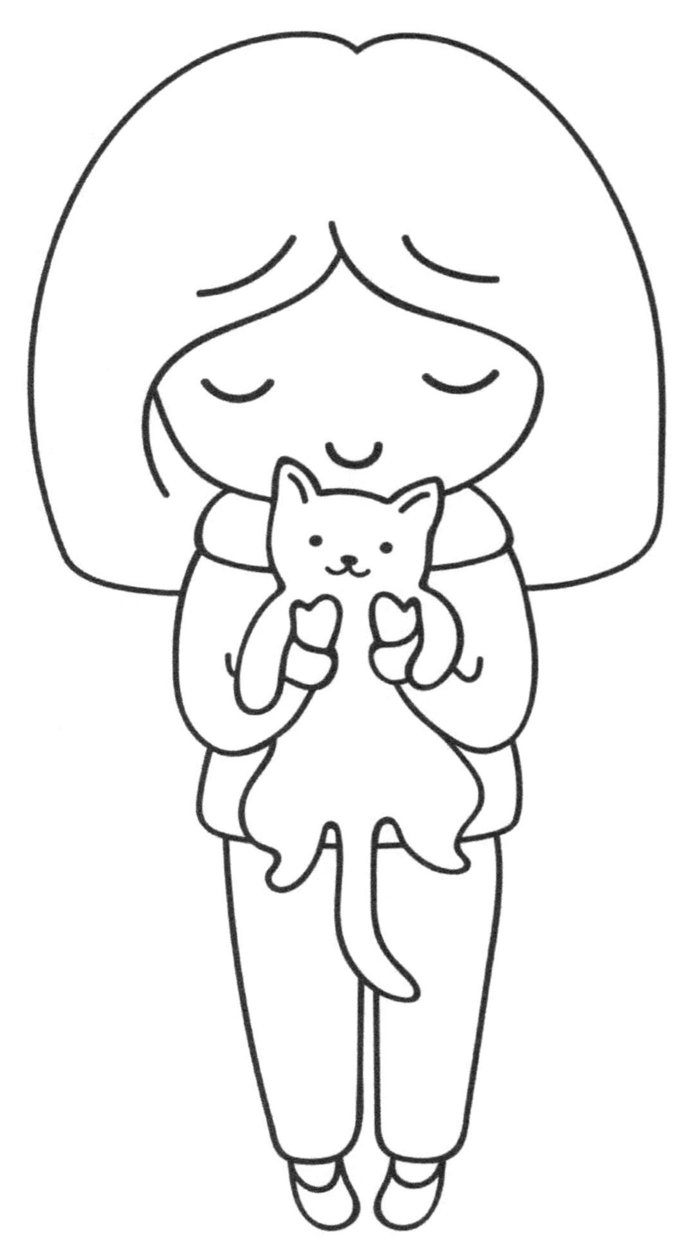

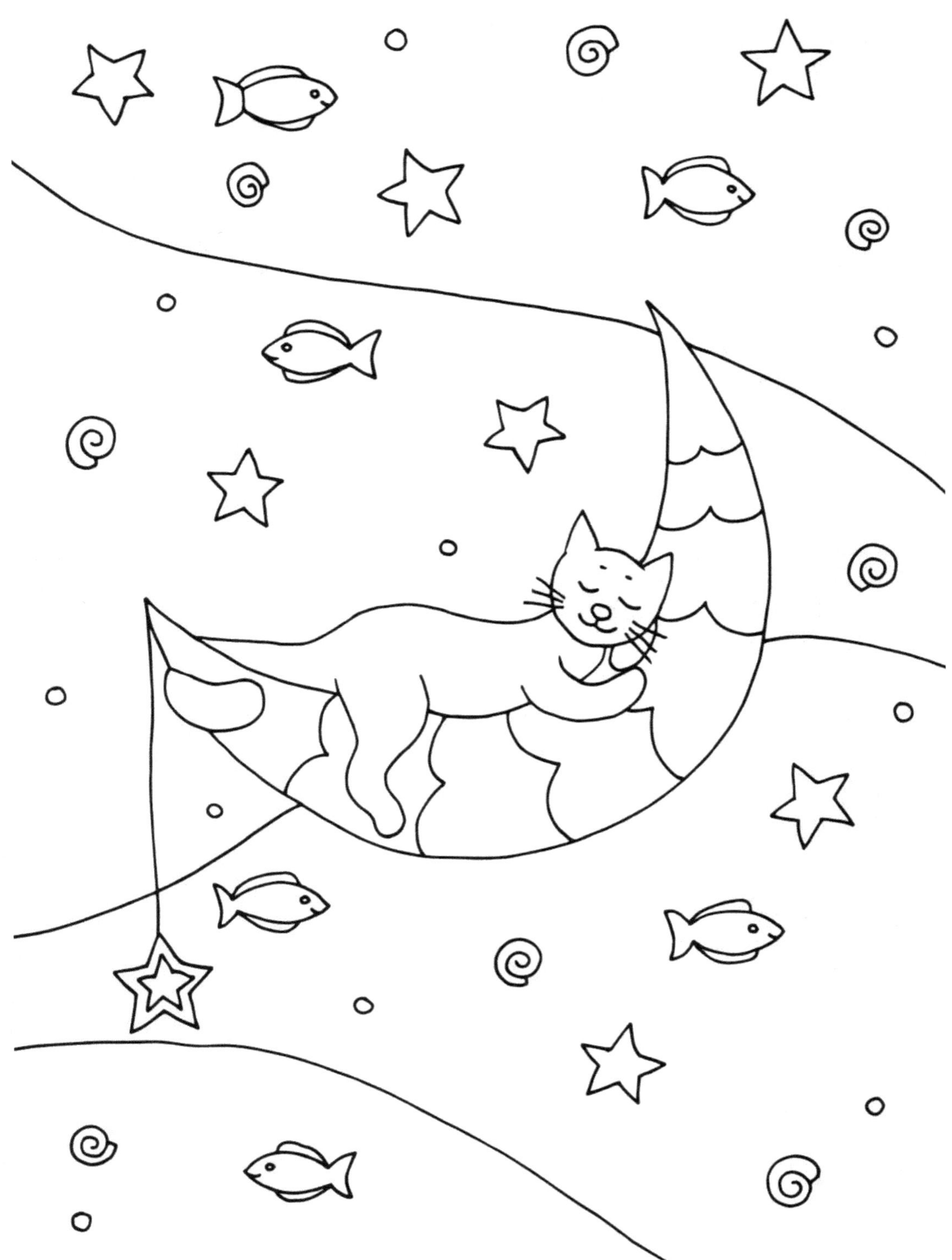

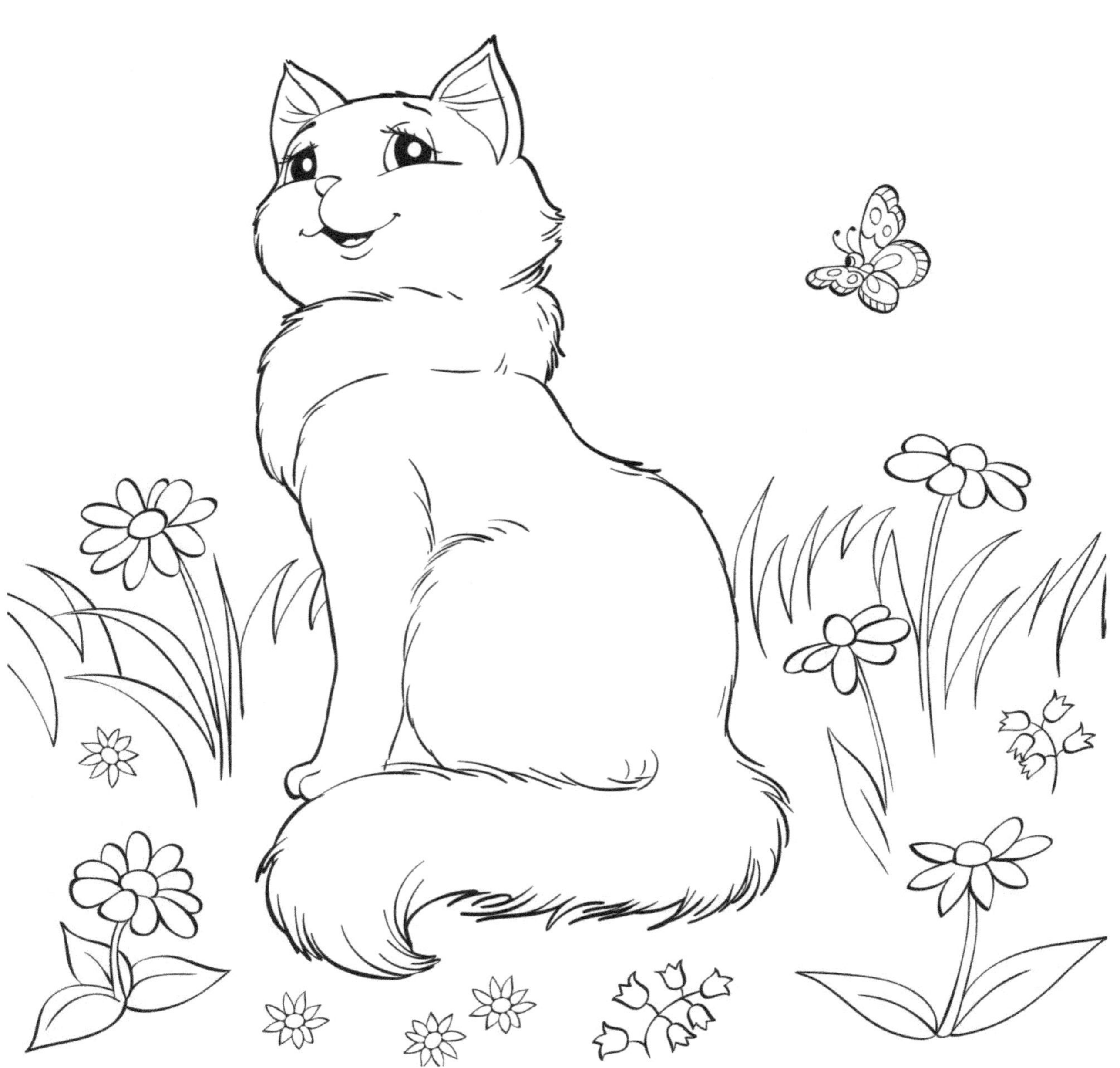

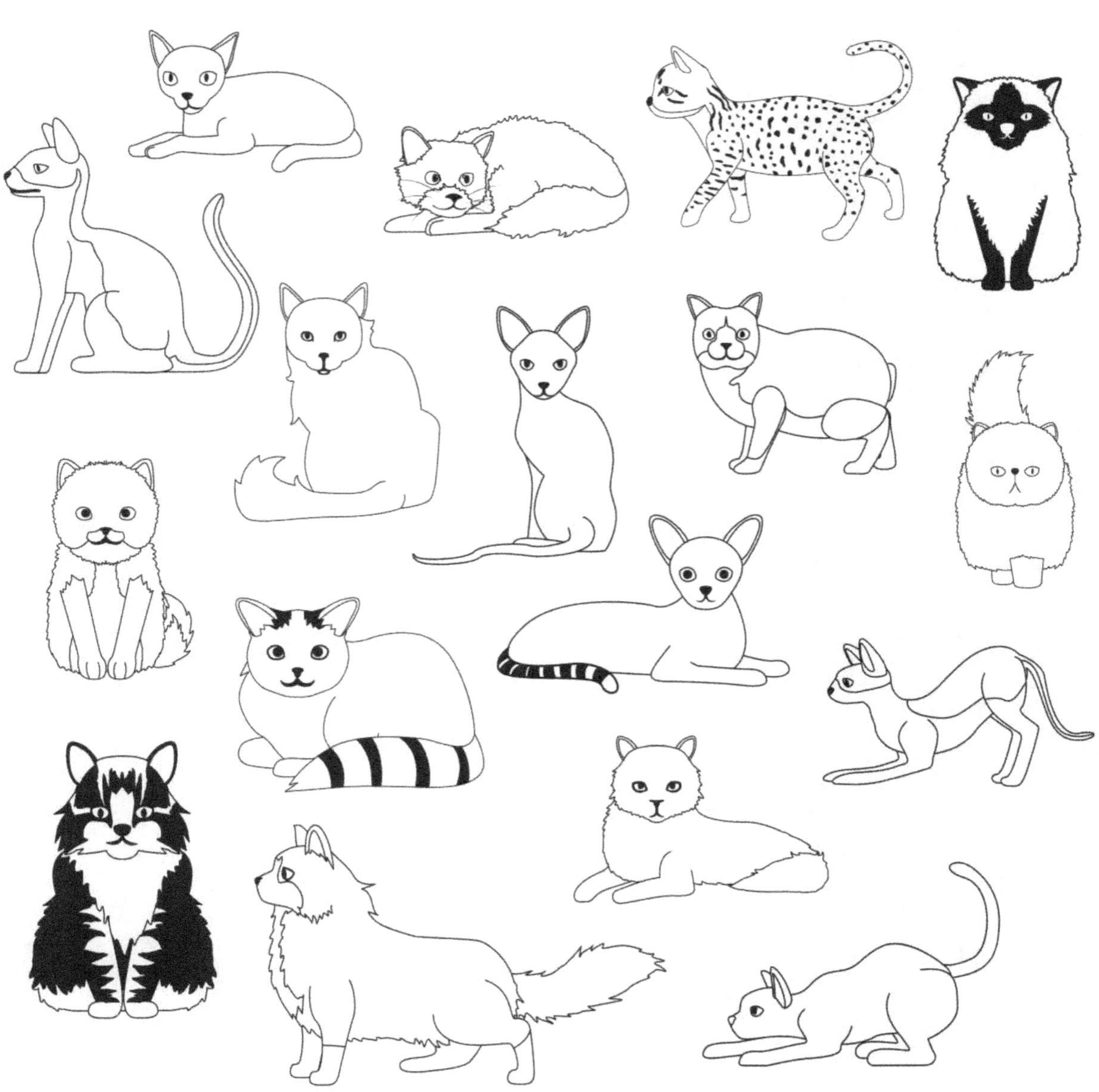

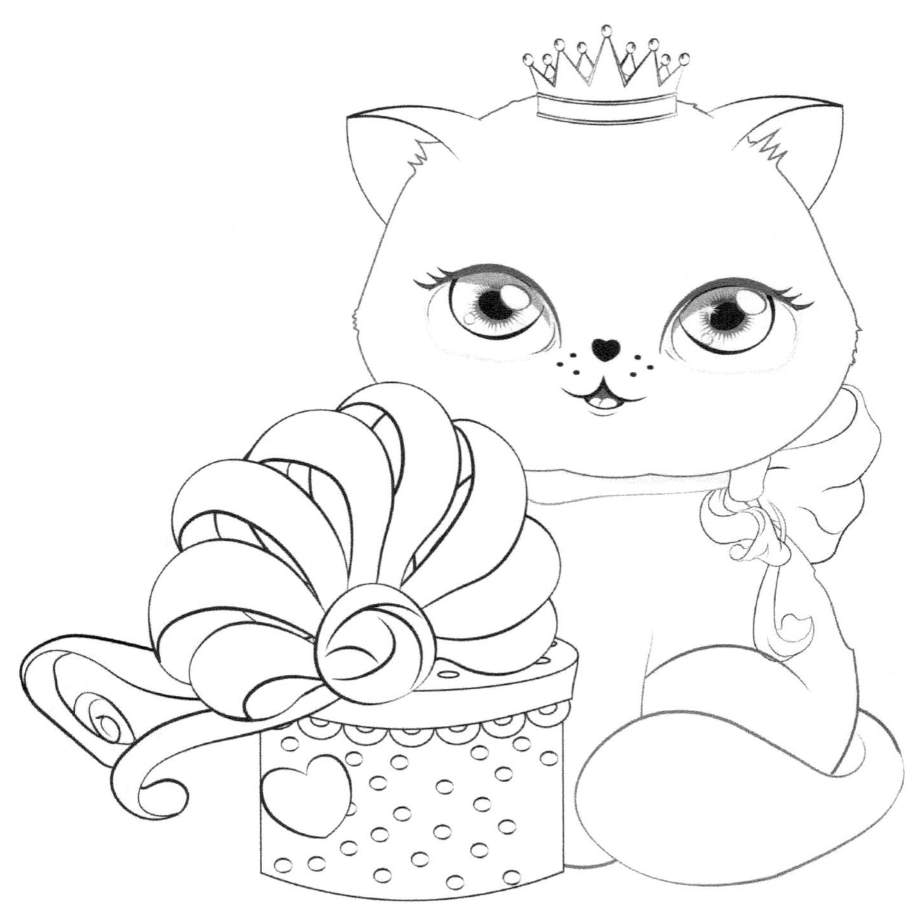

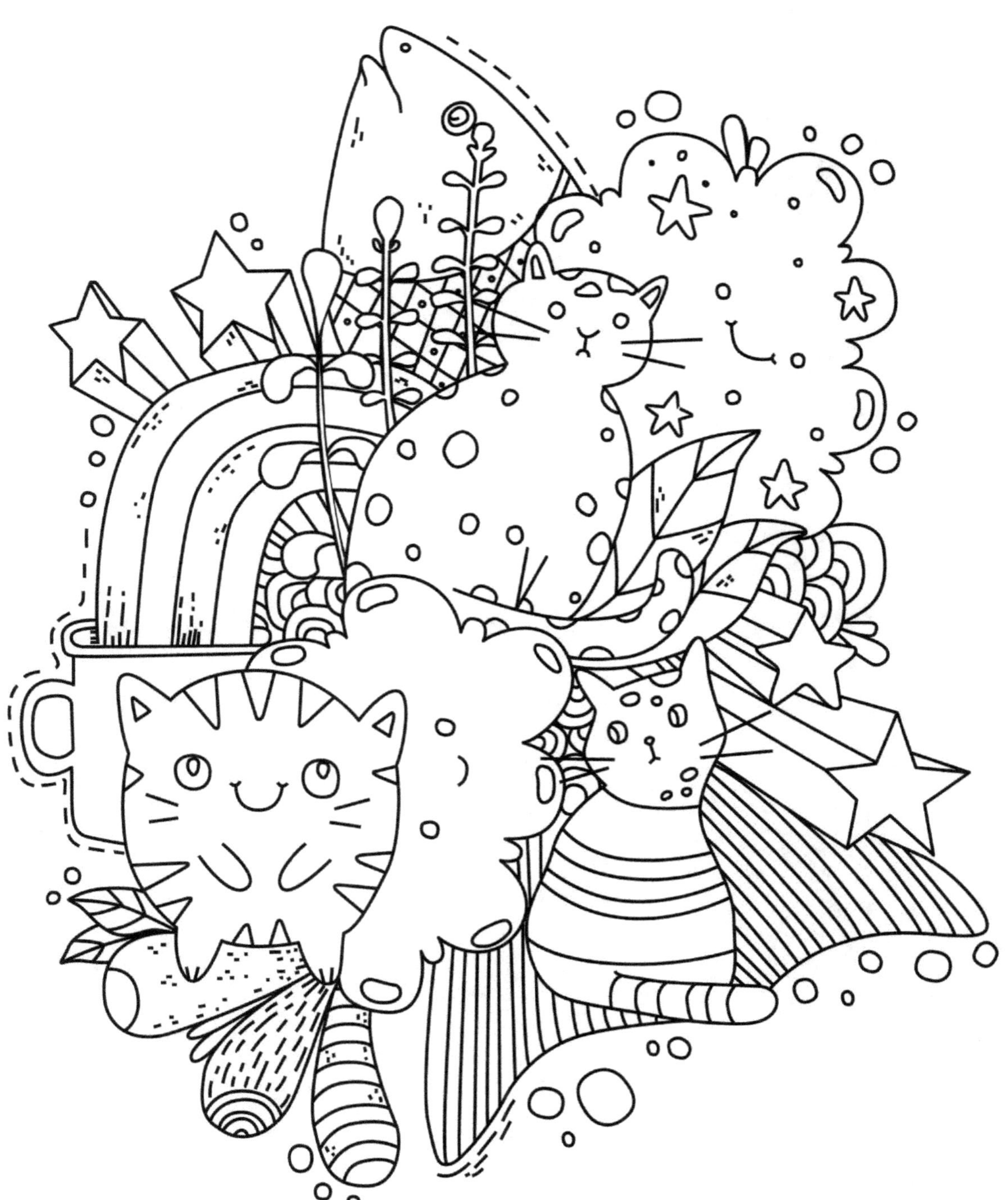

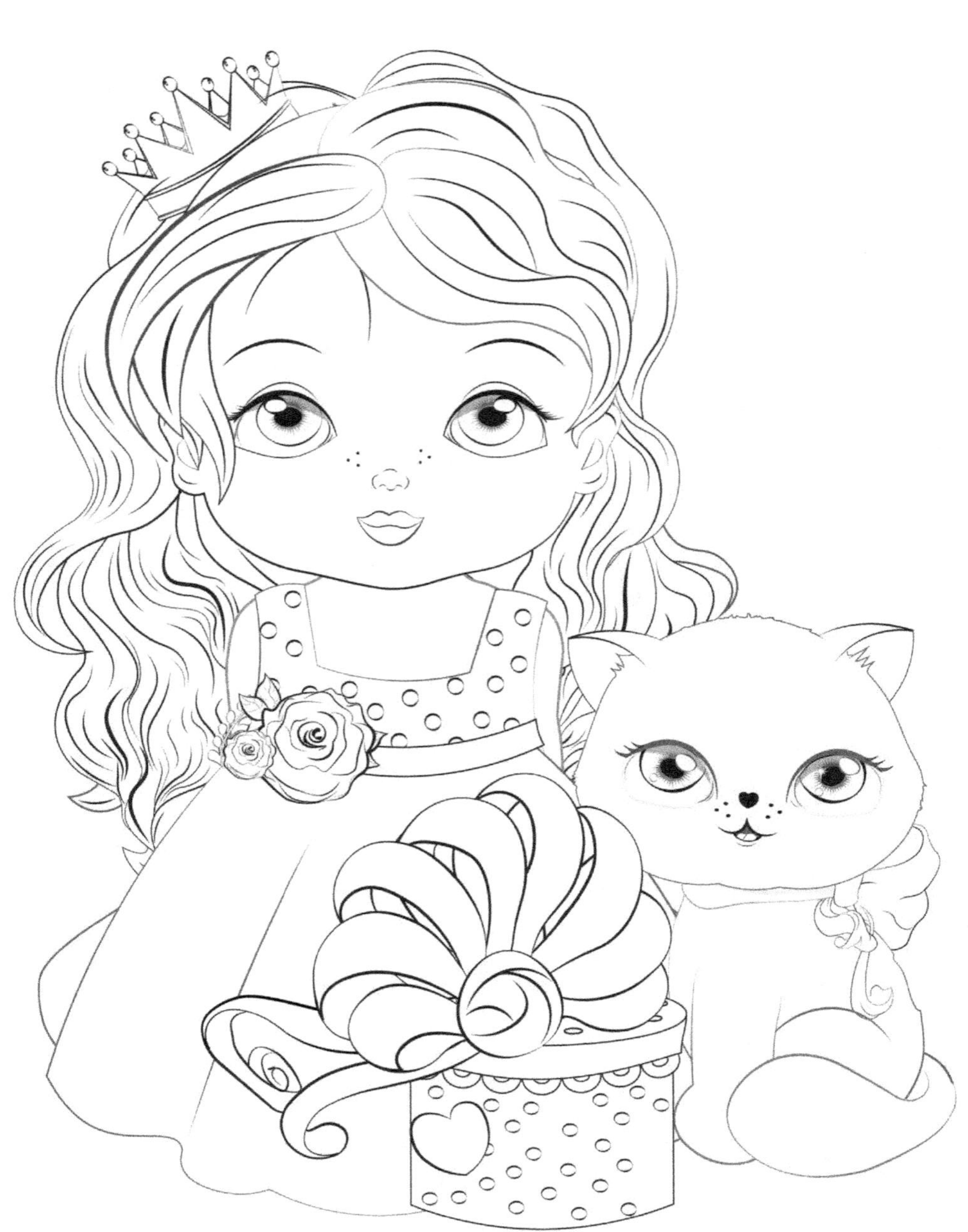

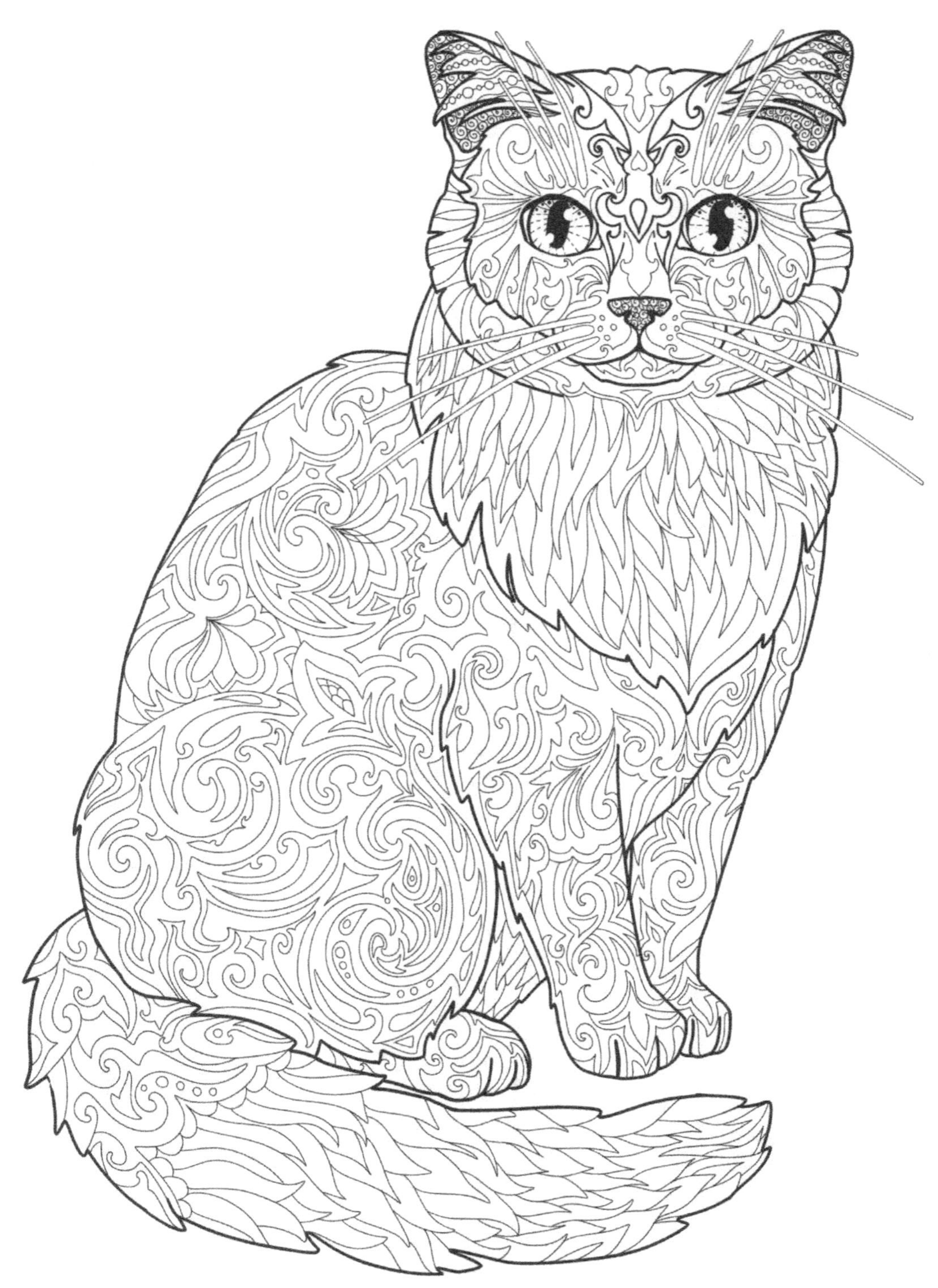

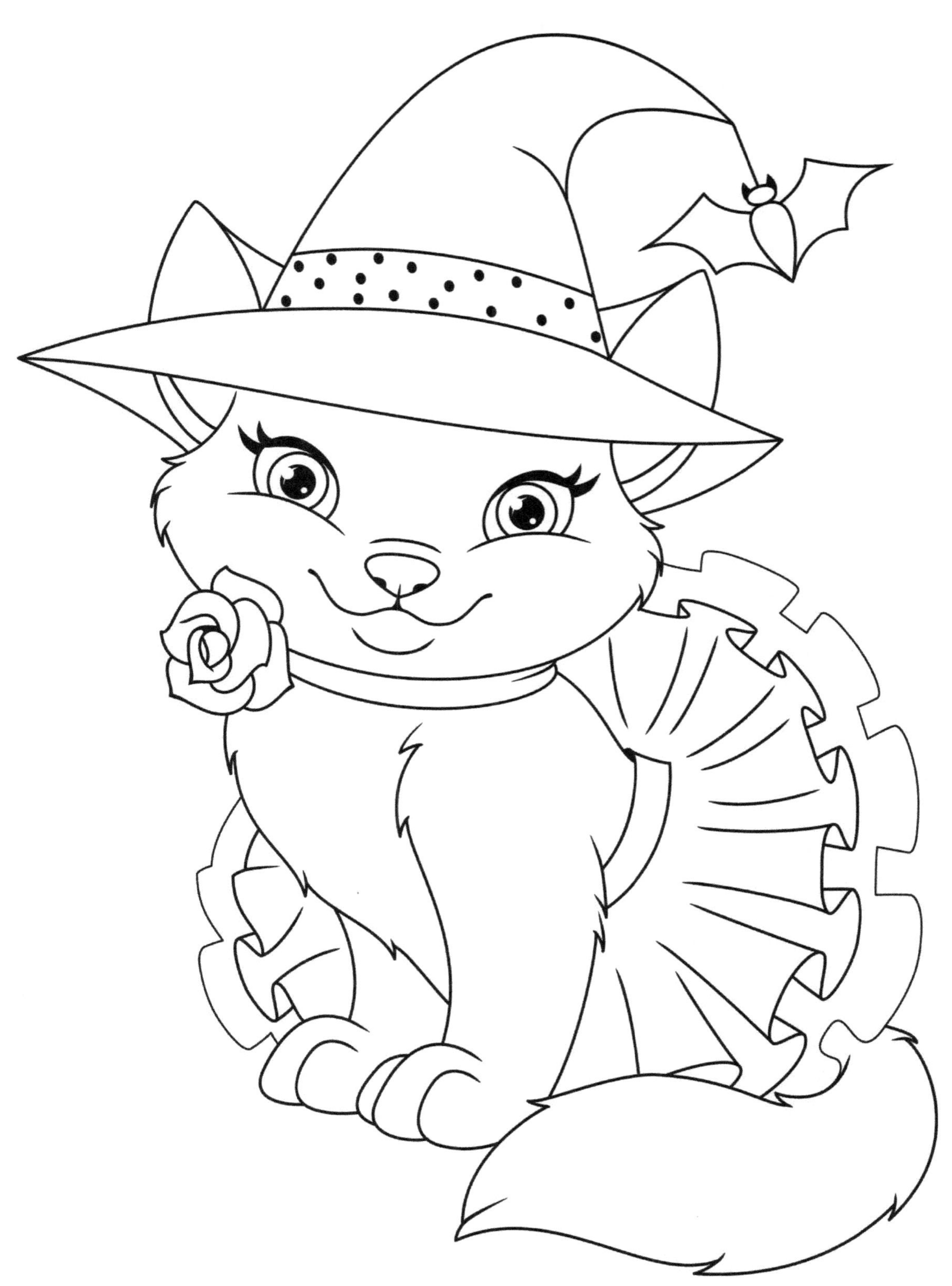

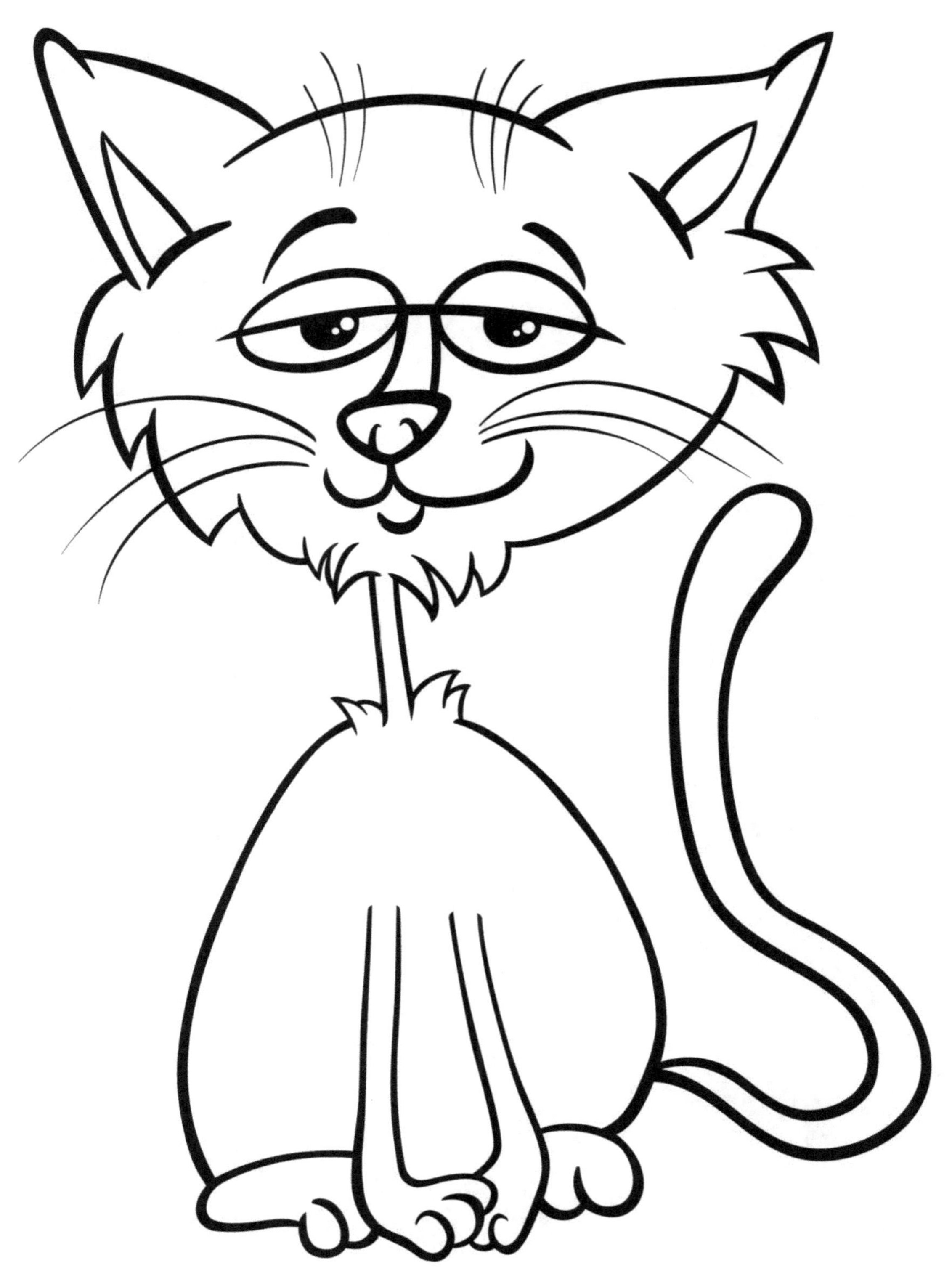

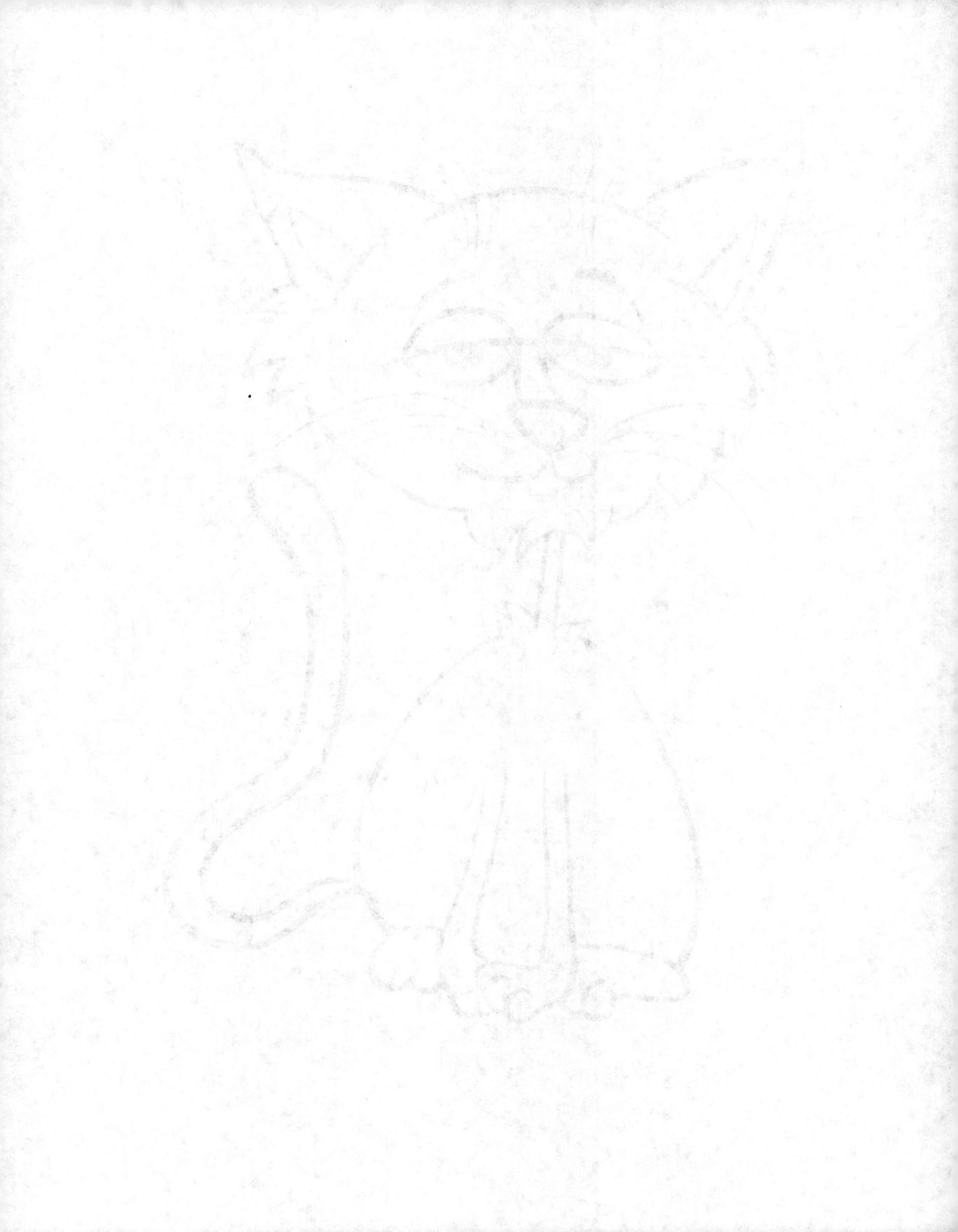

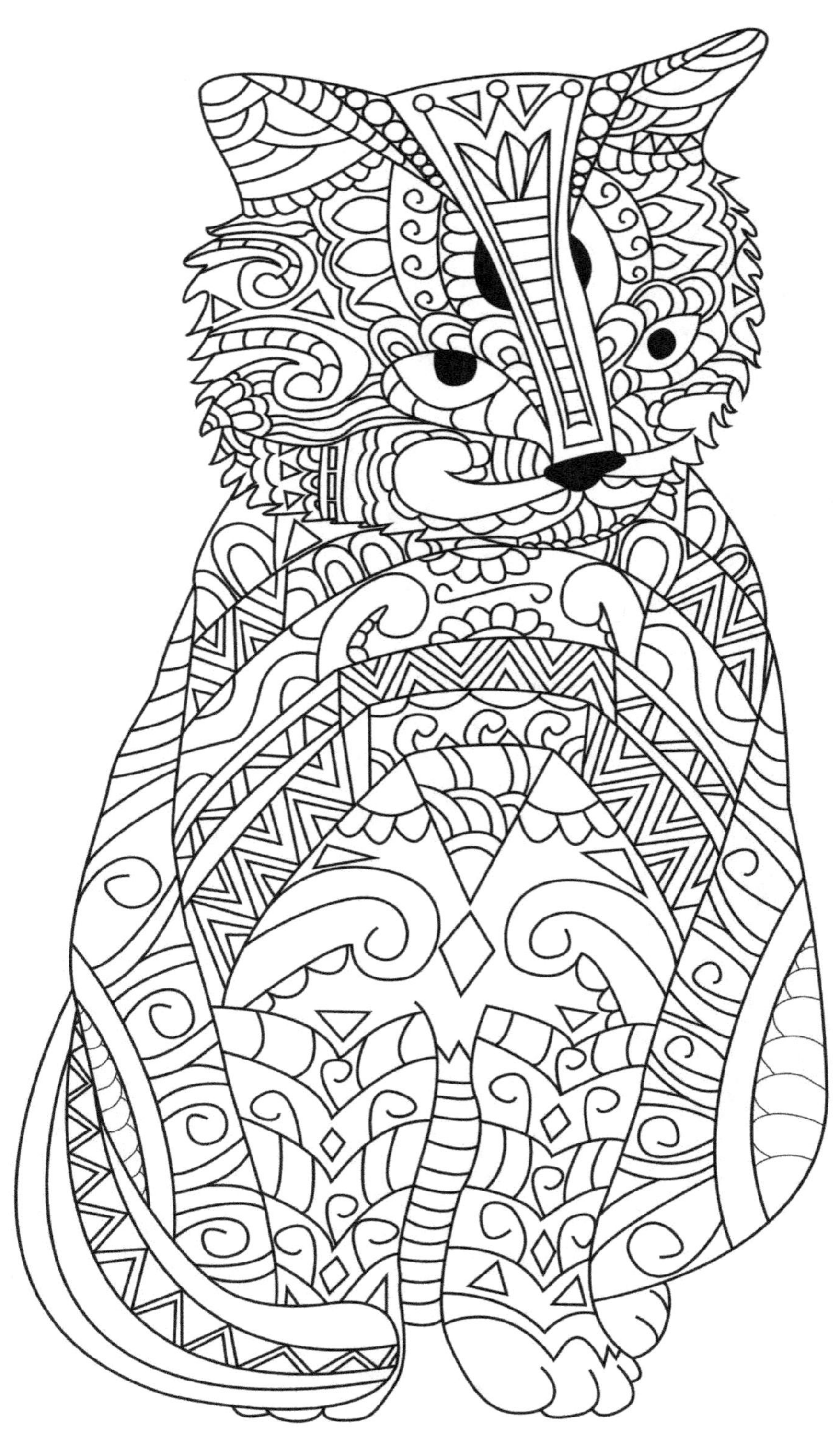

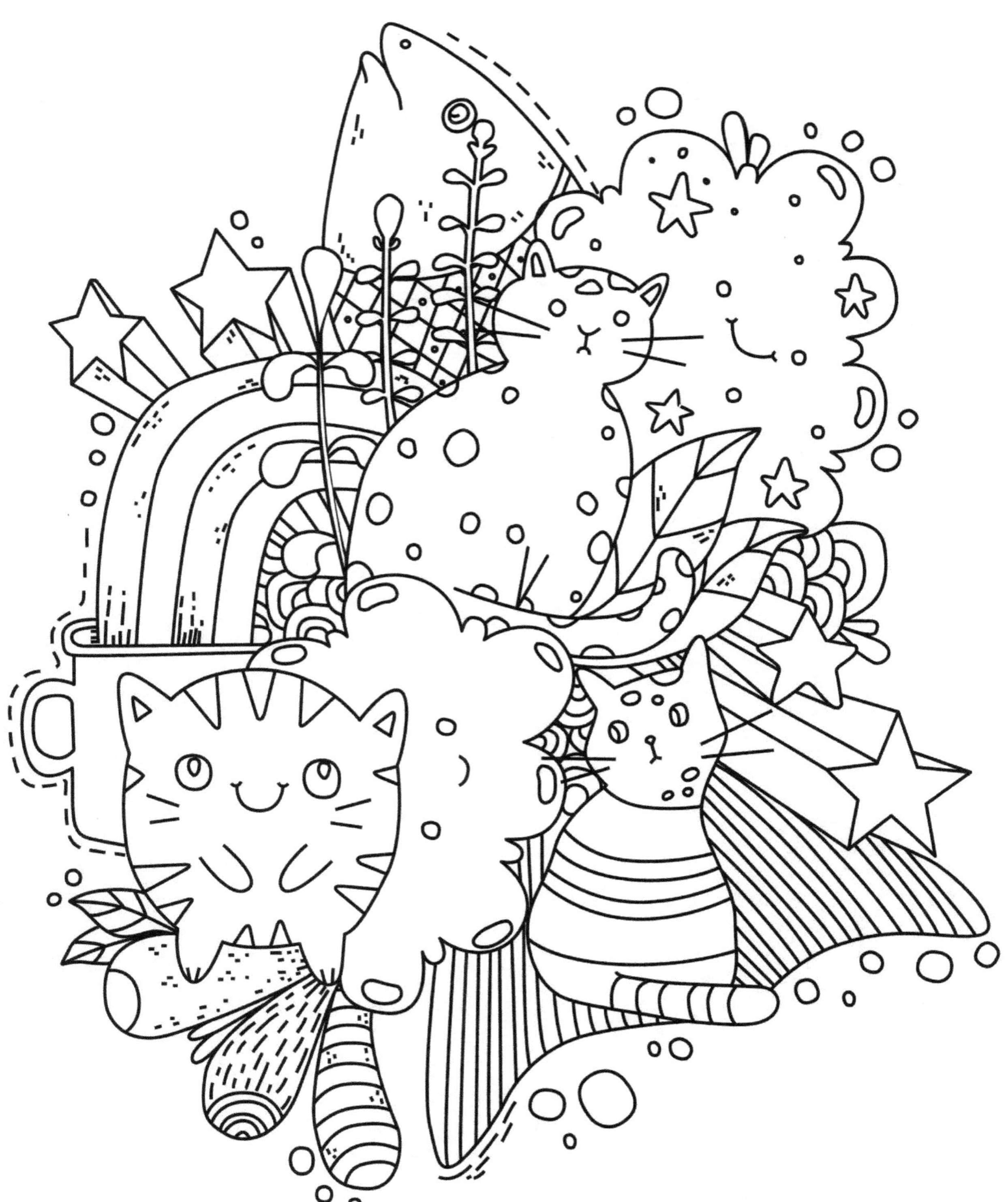

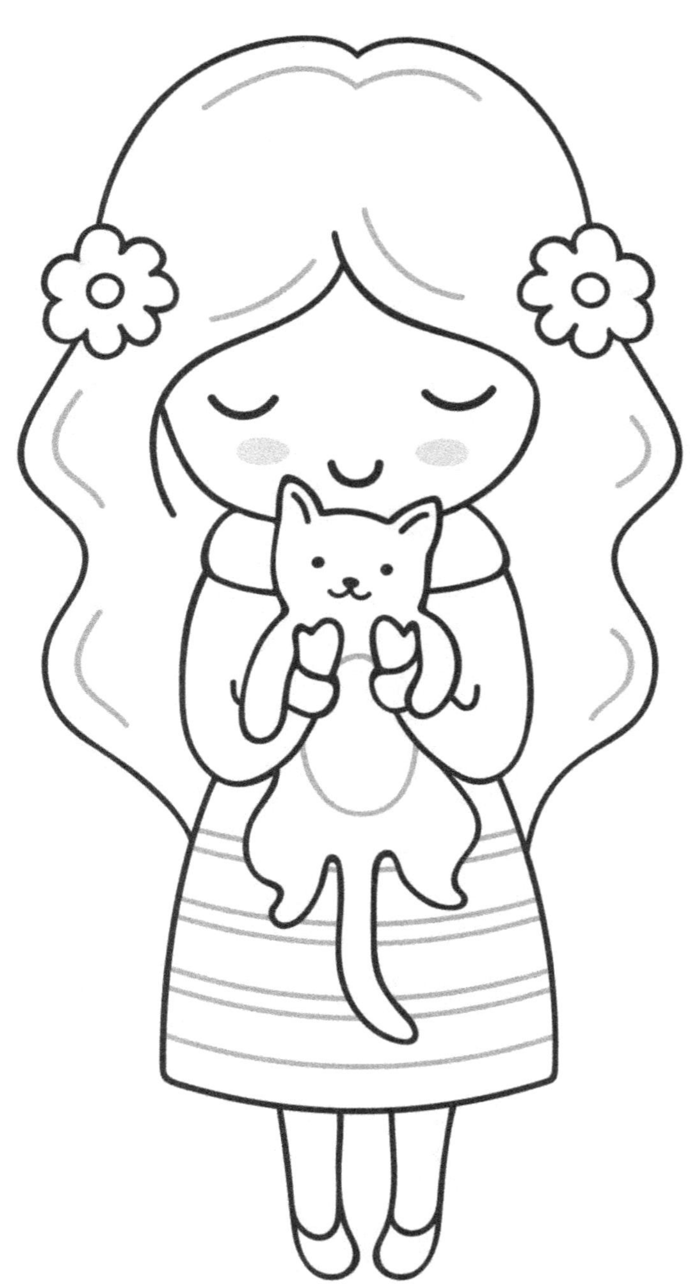

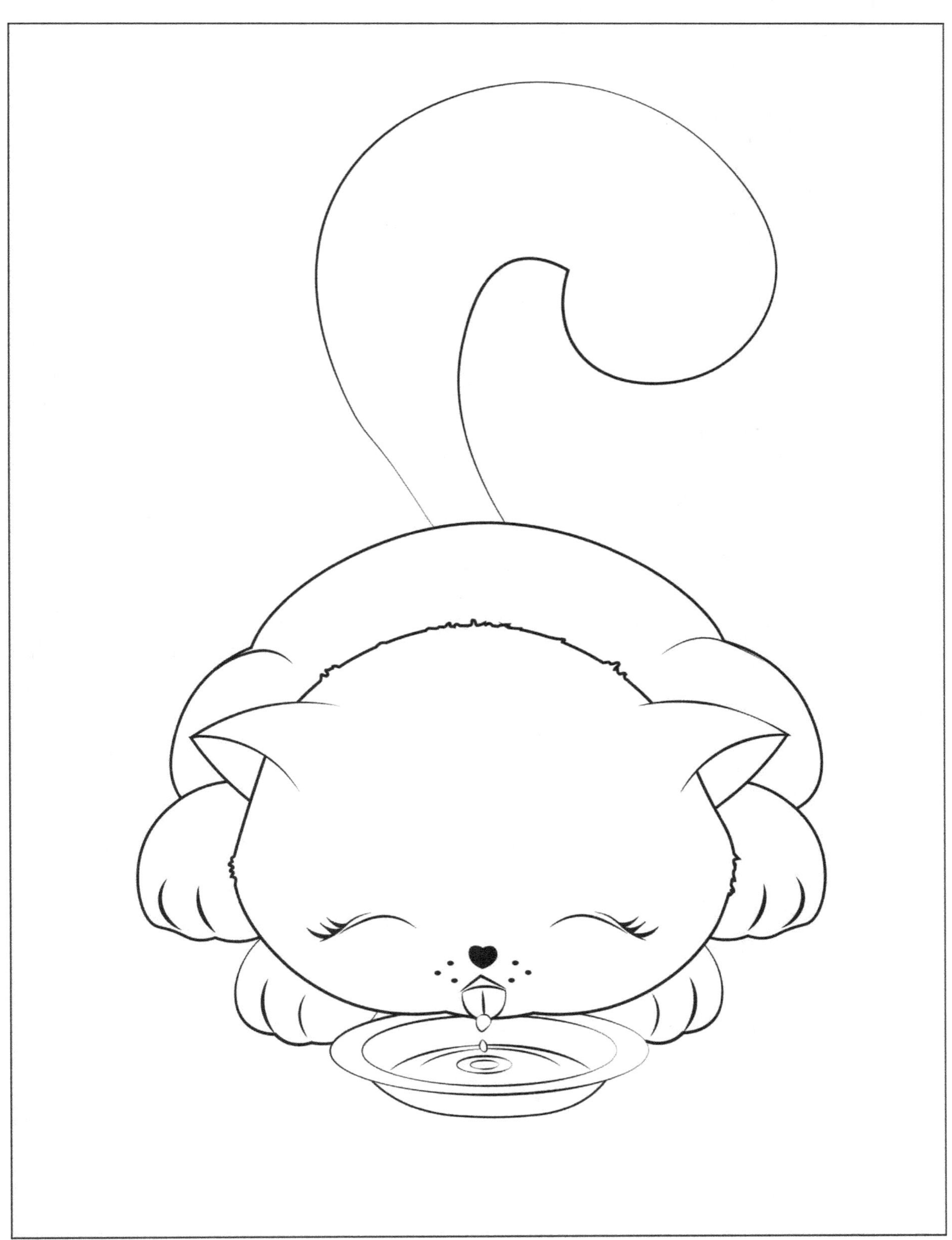

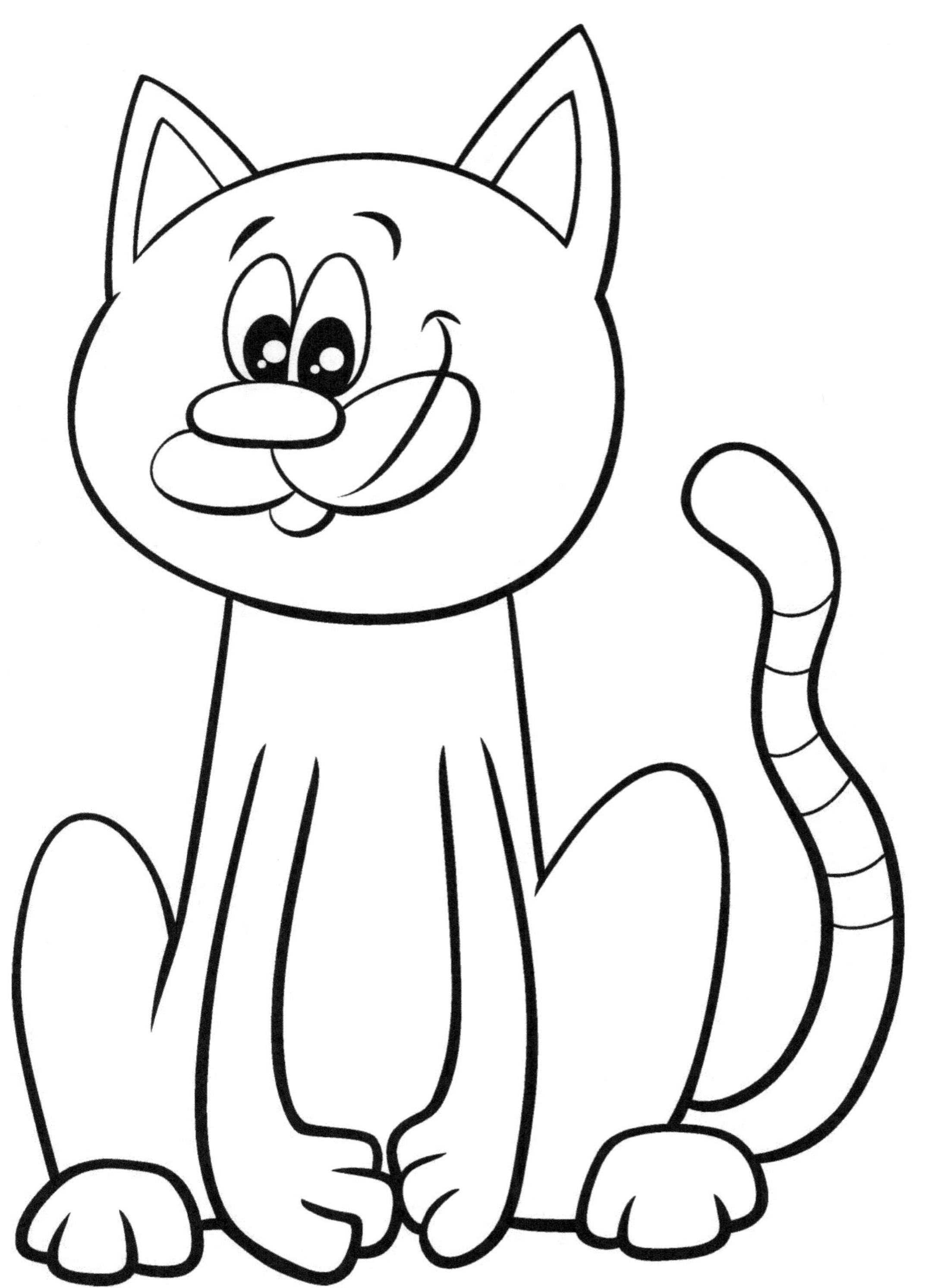

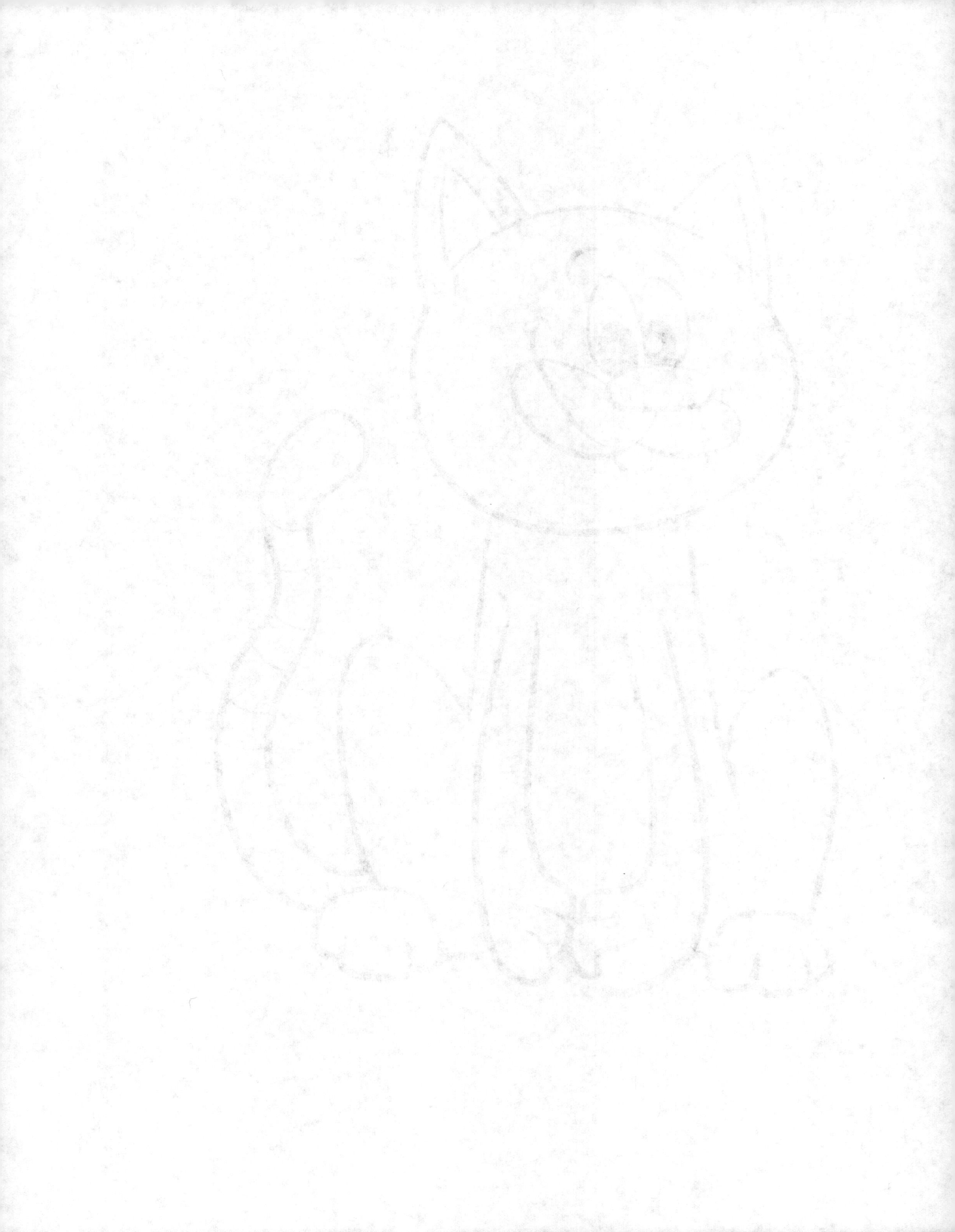

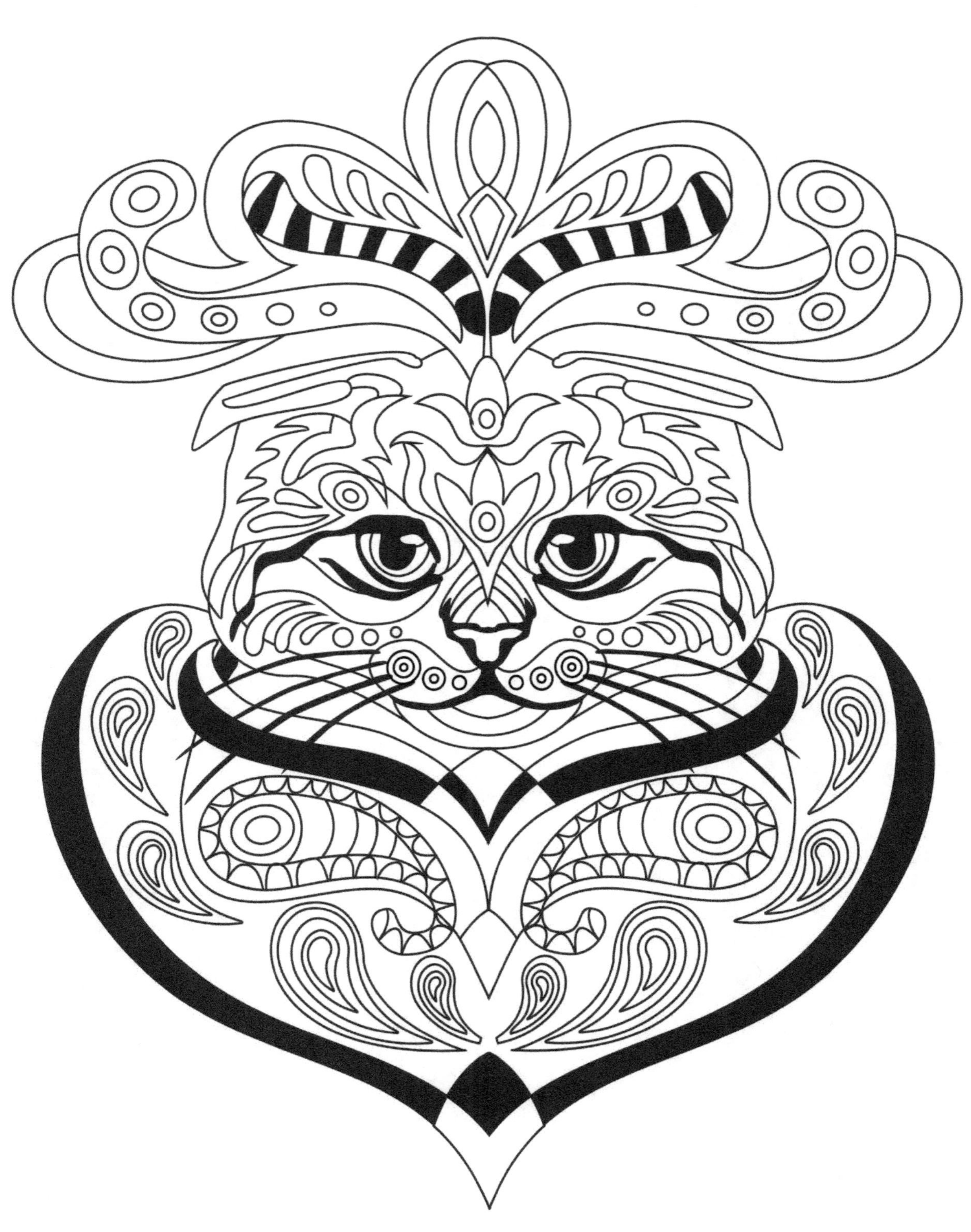

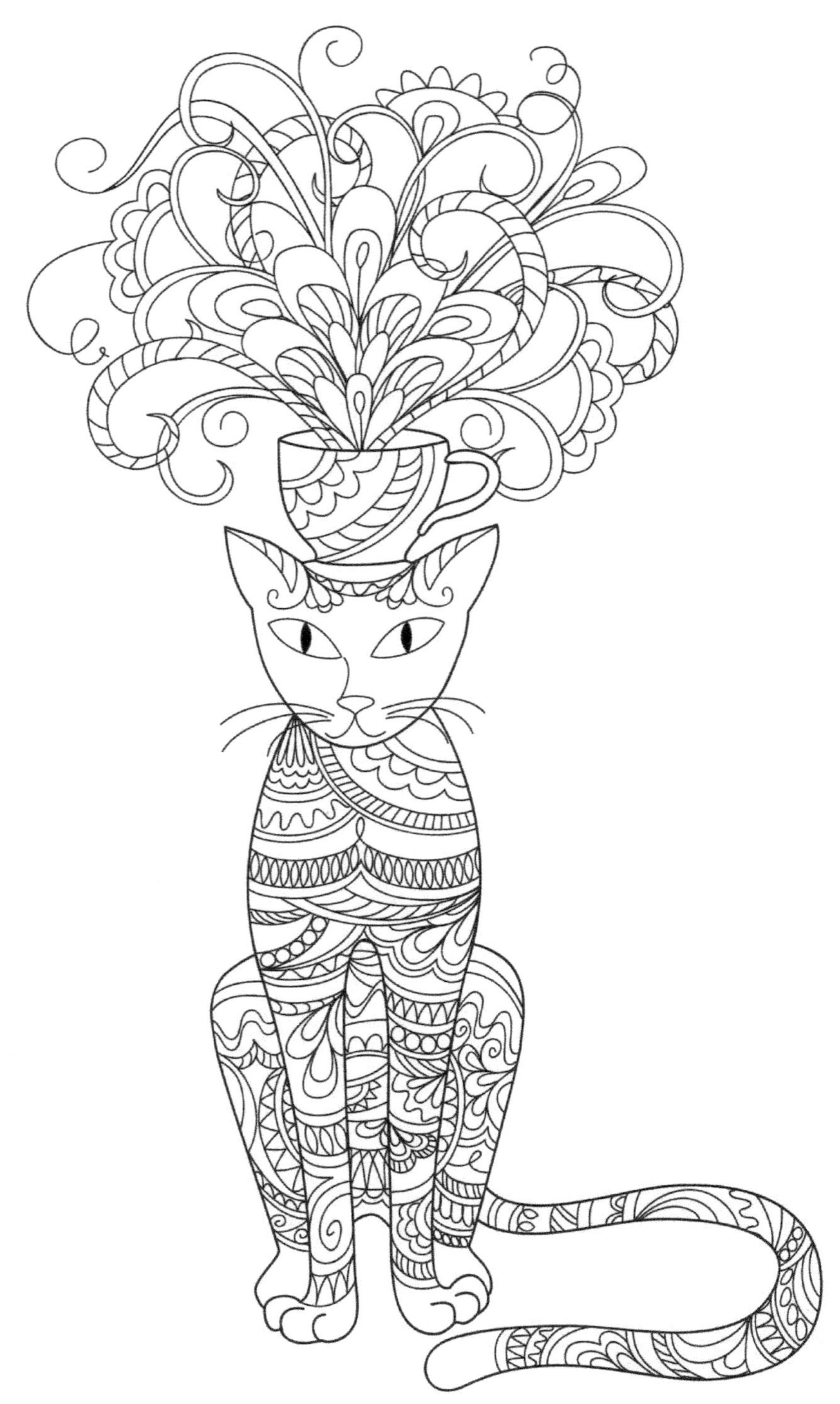

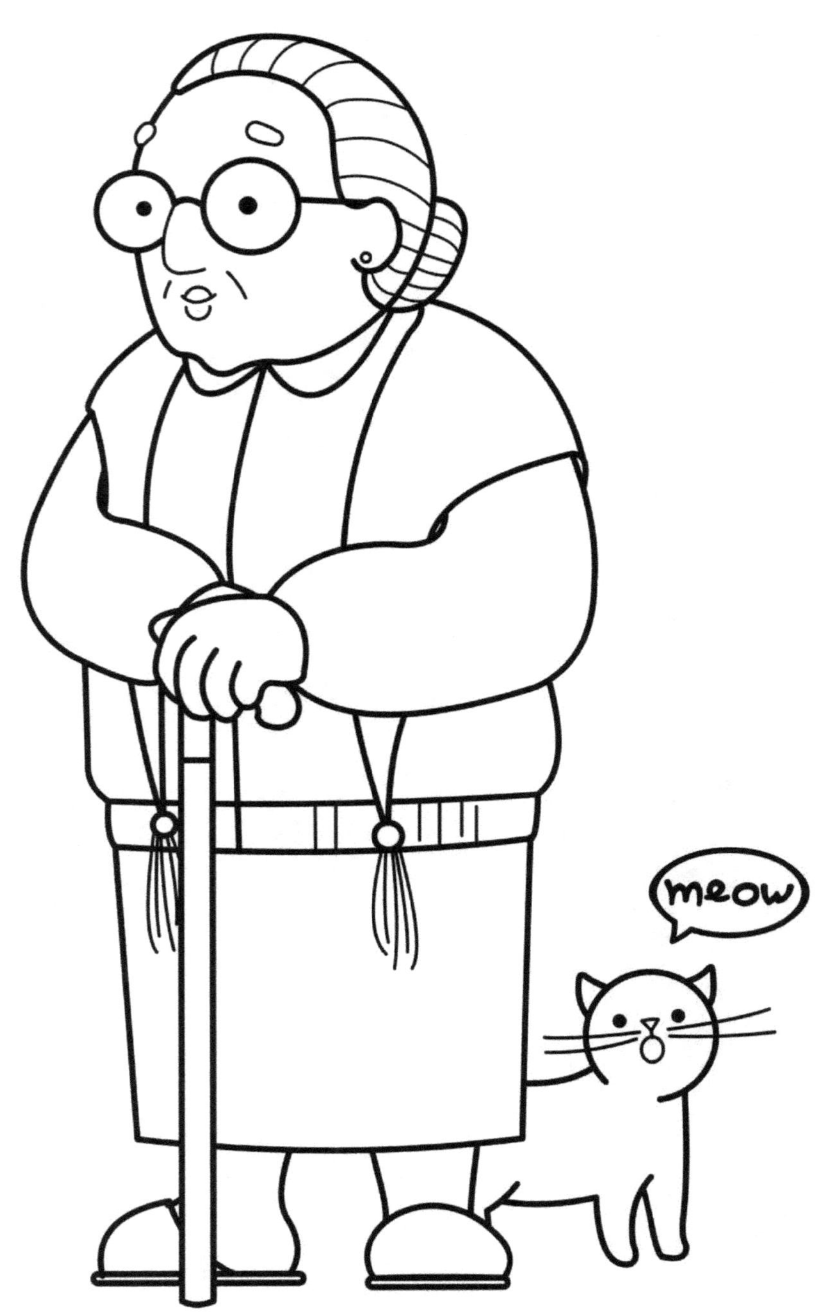
meow

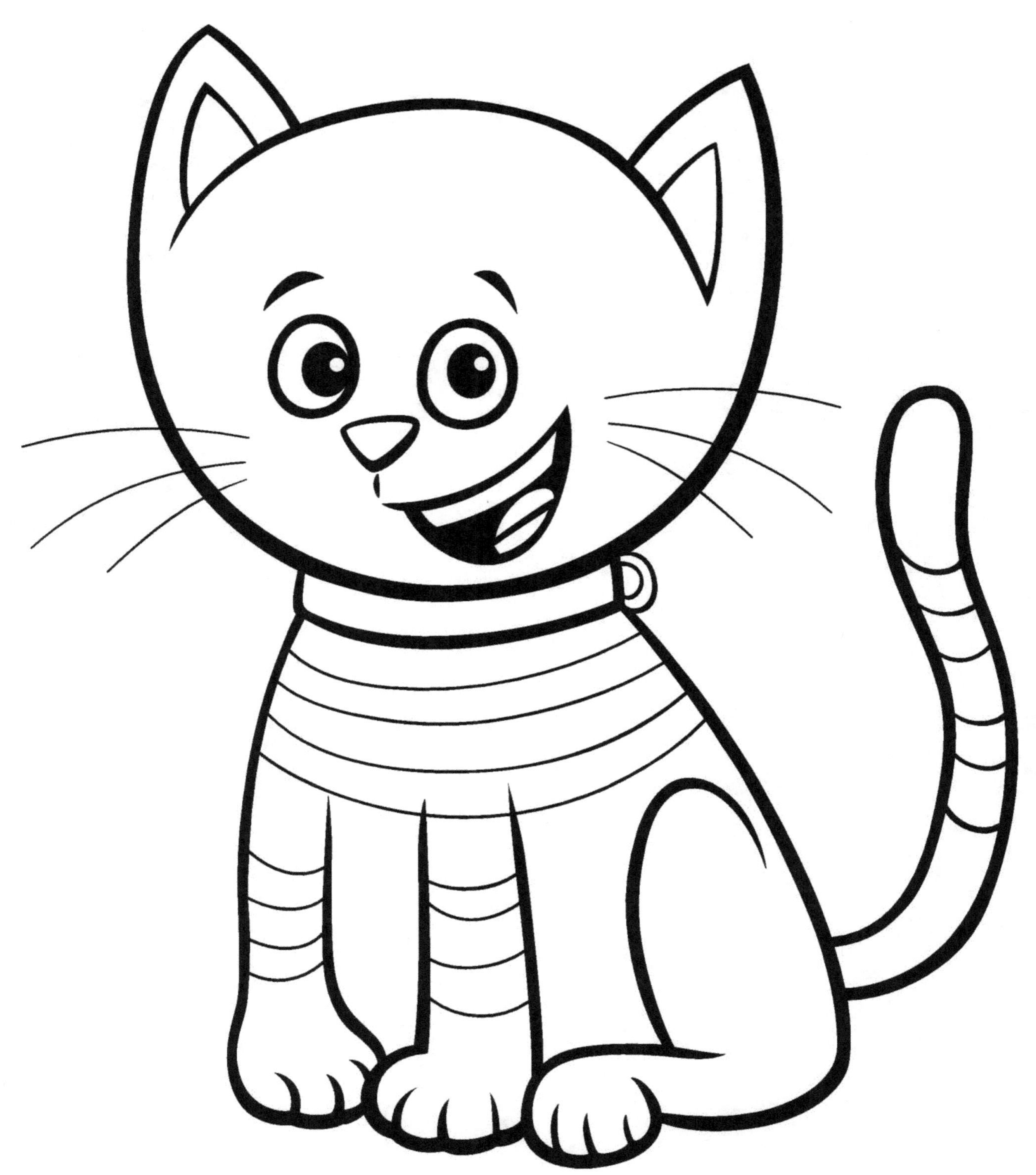

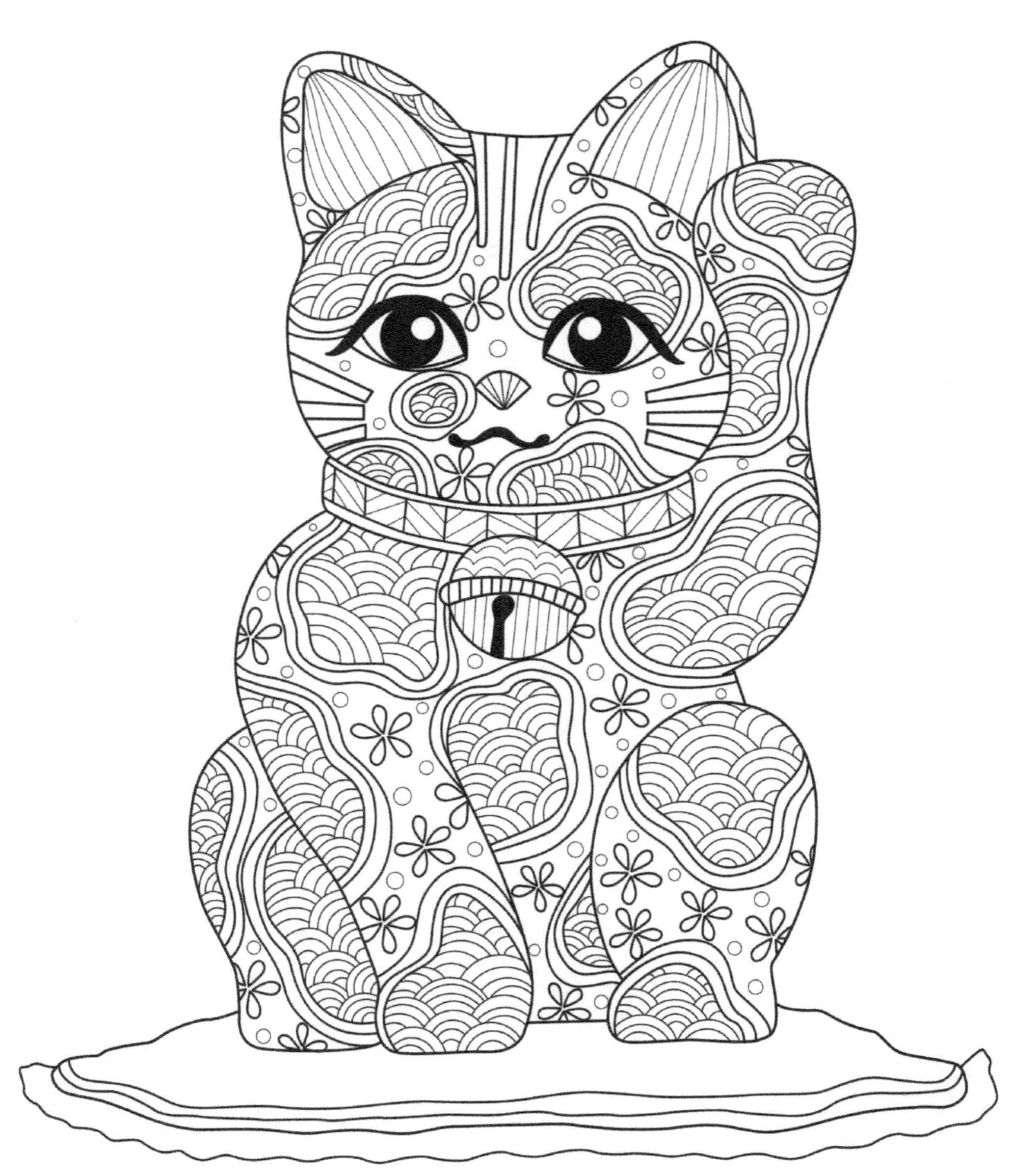

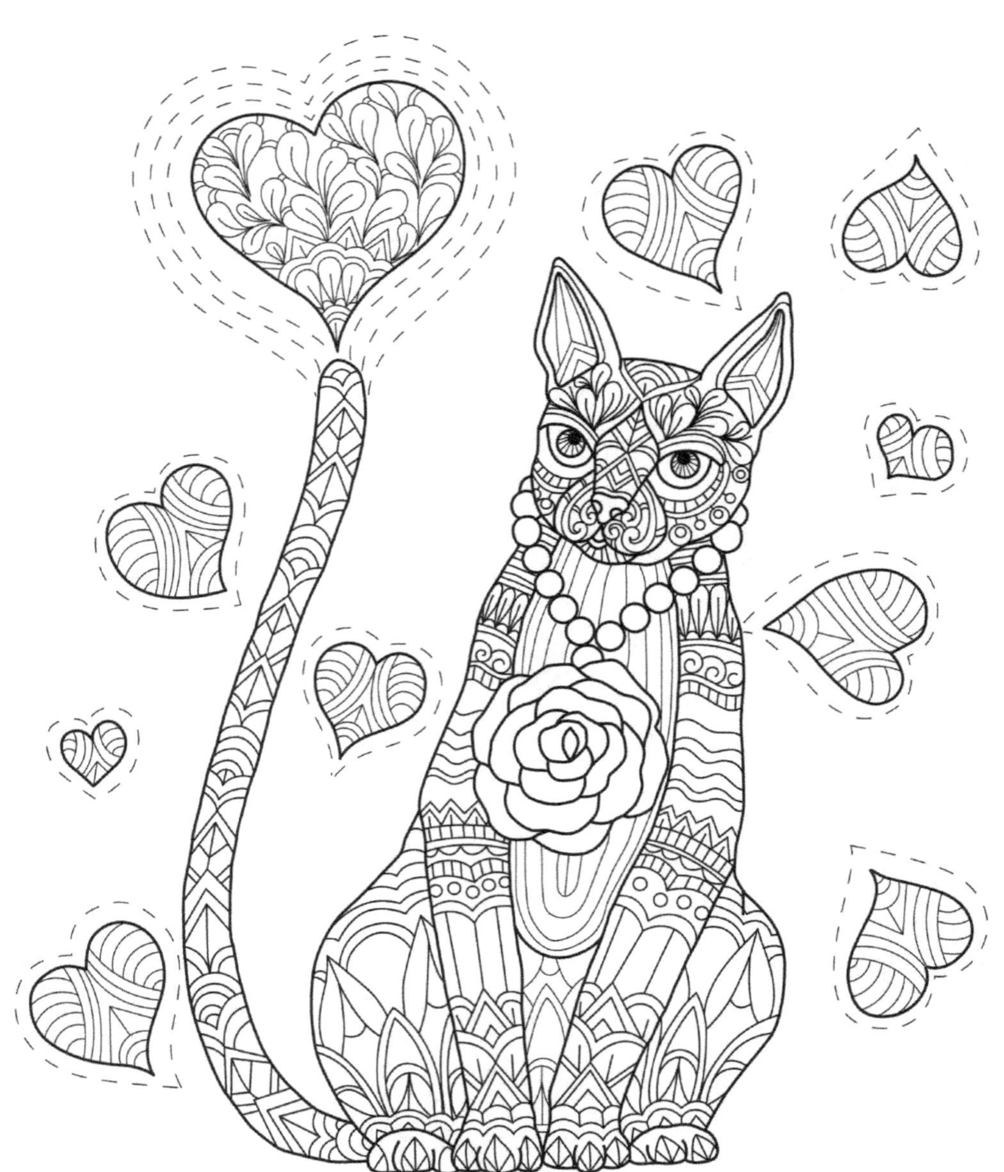

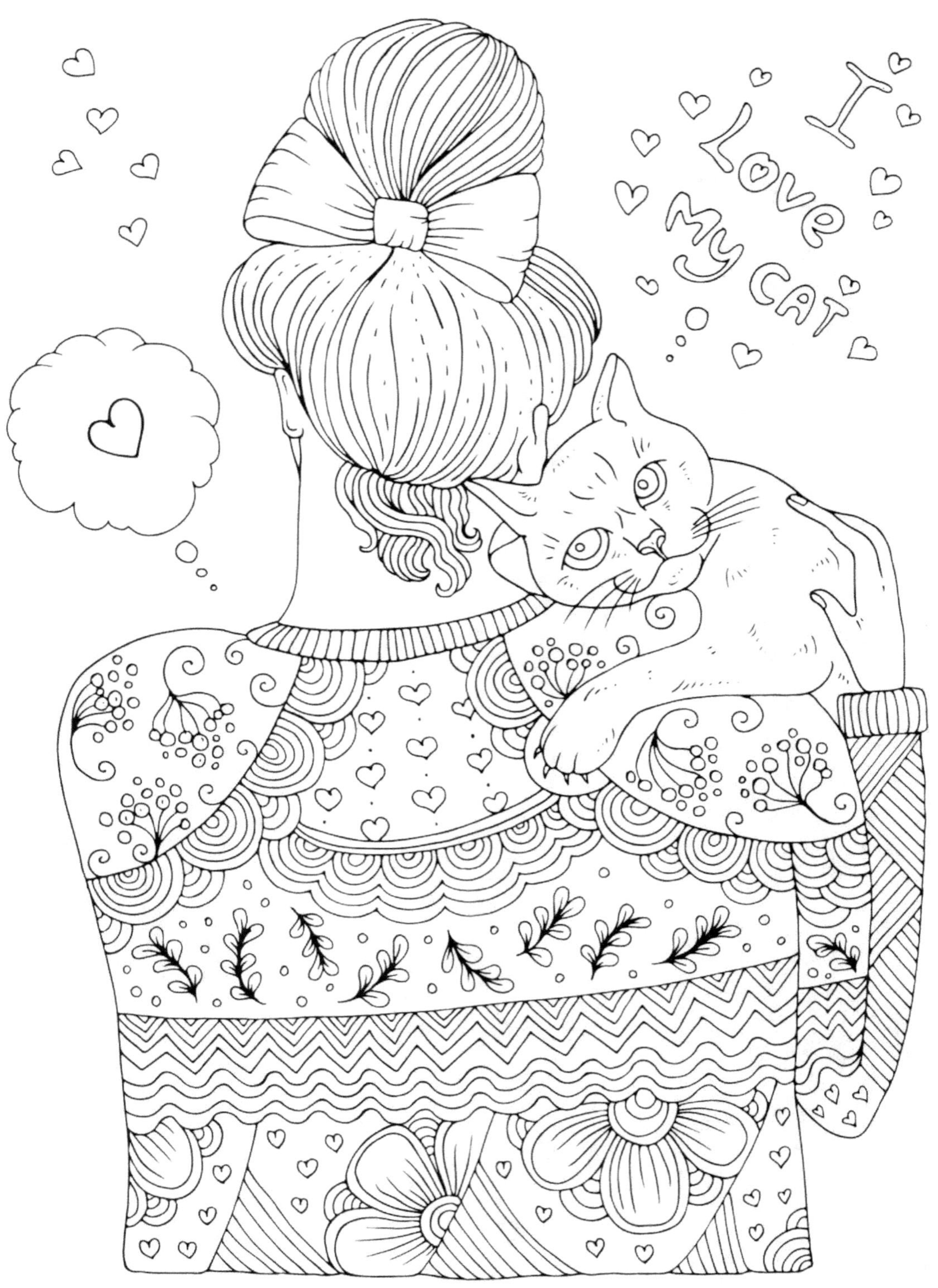
I Love My CAT

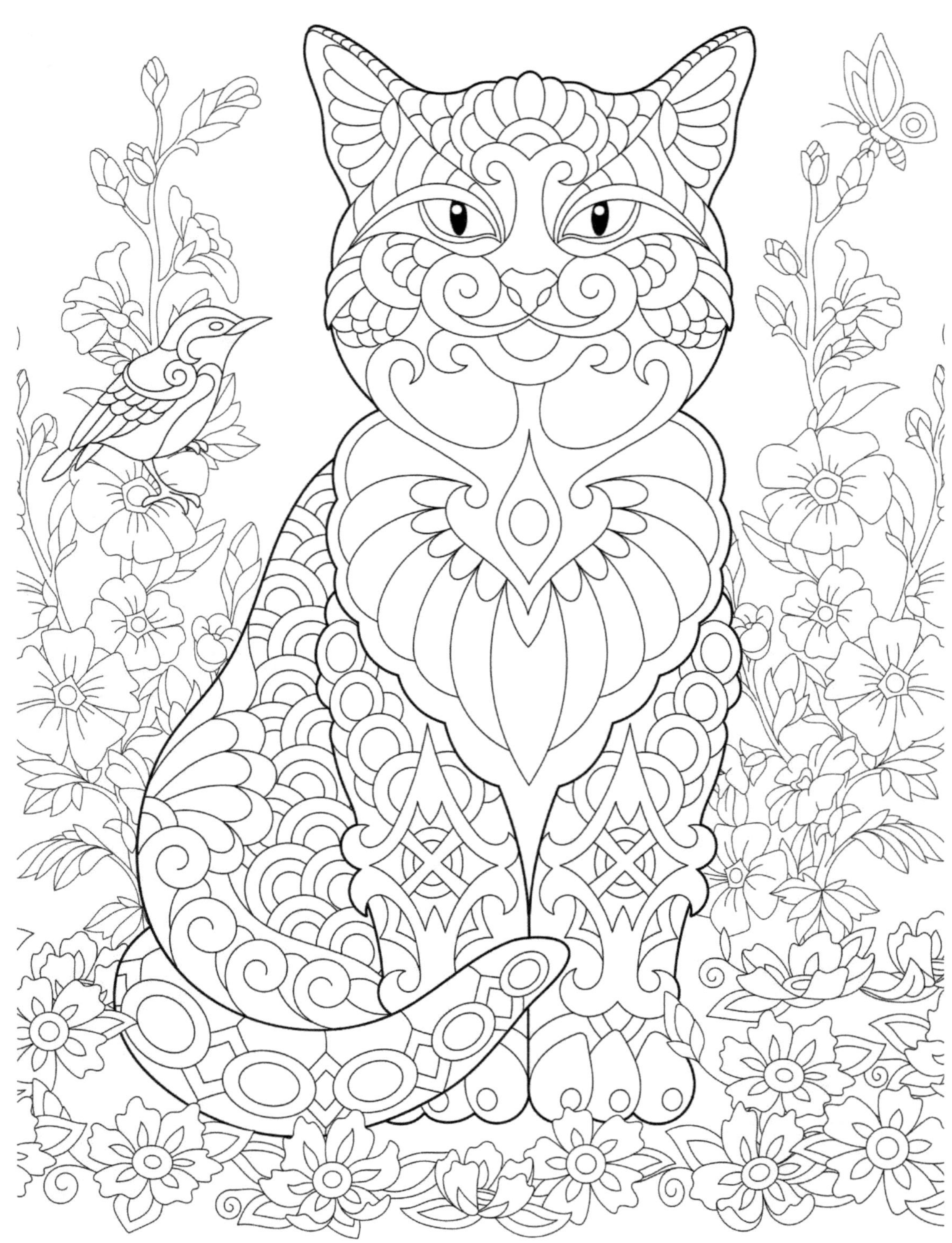

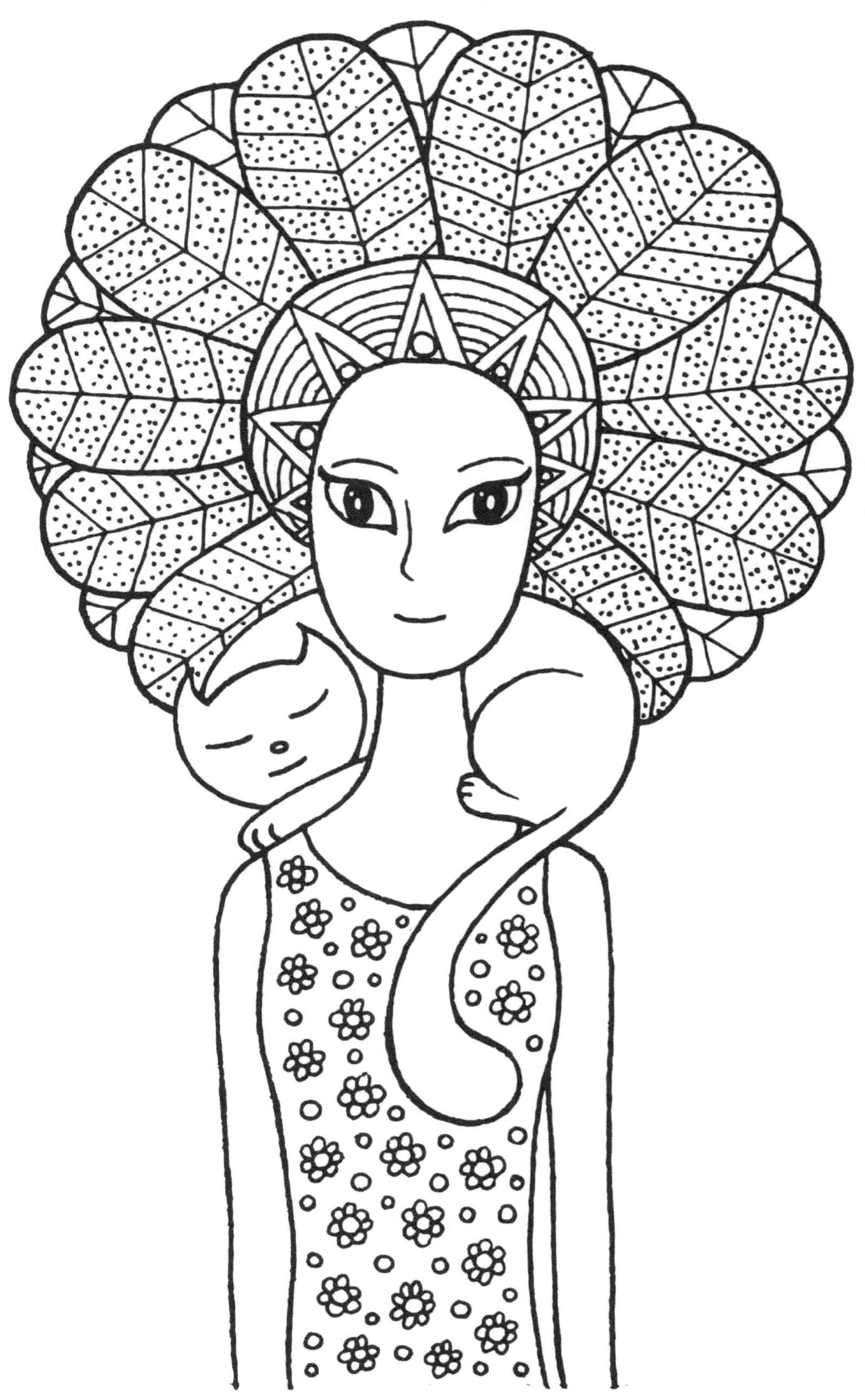

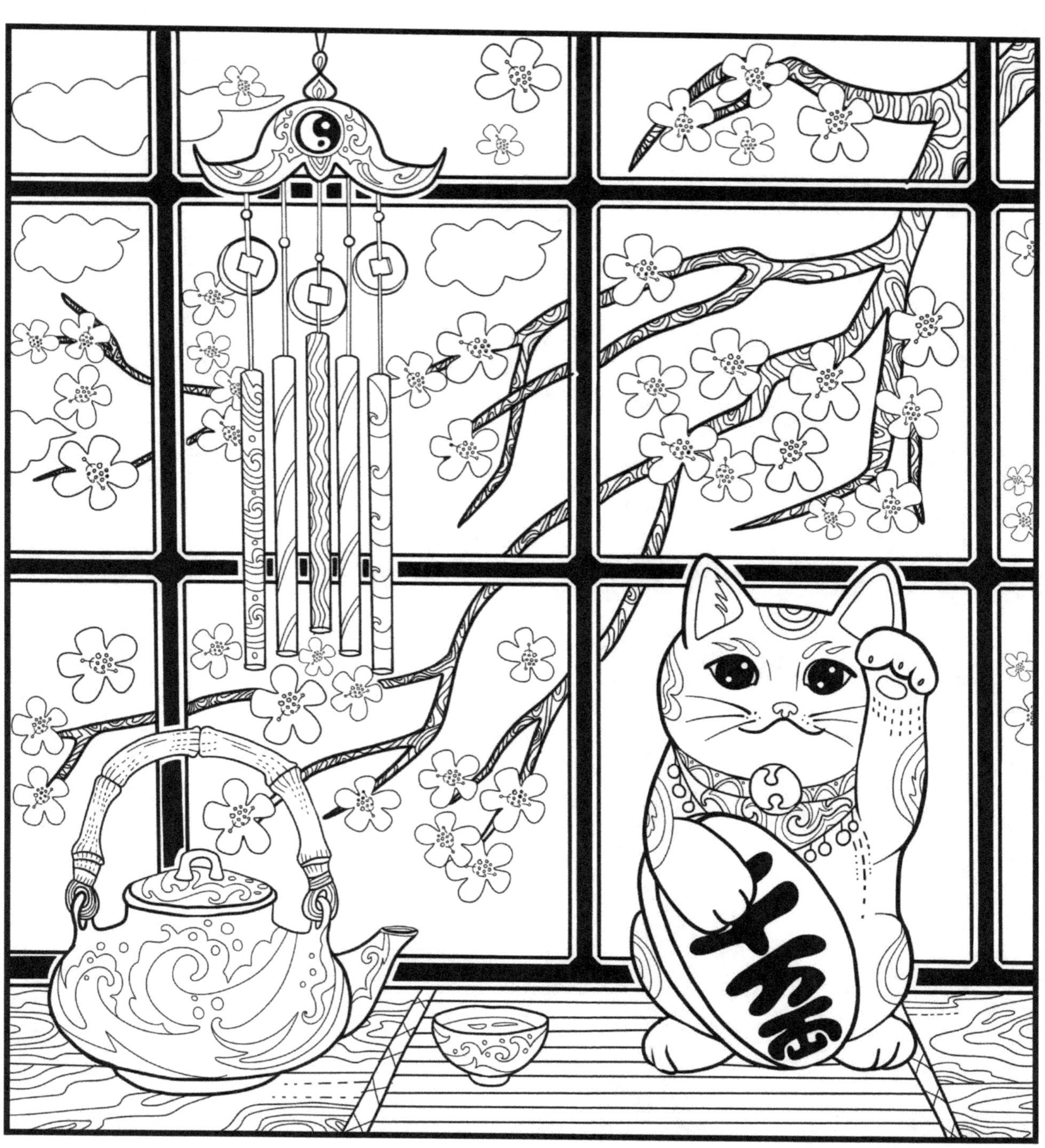

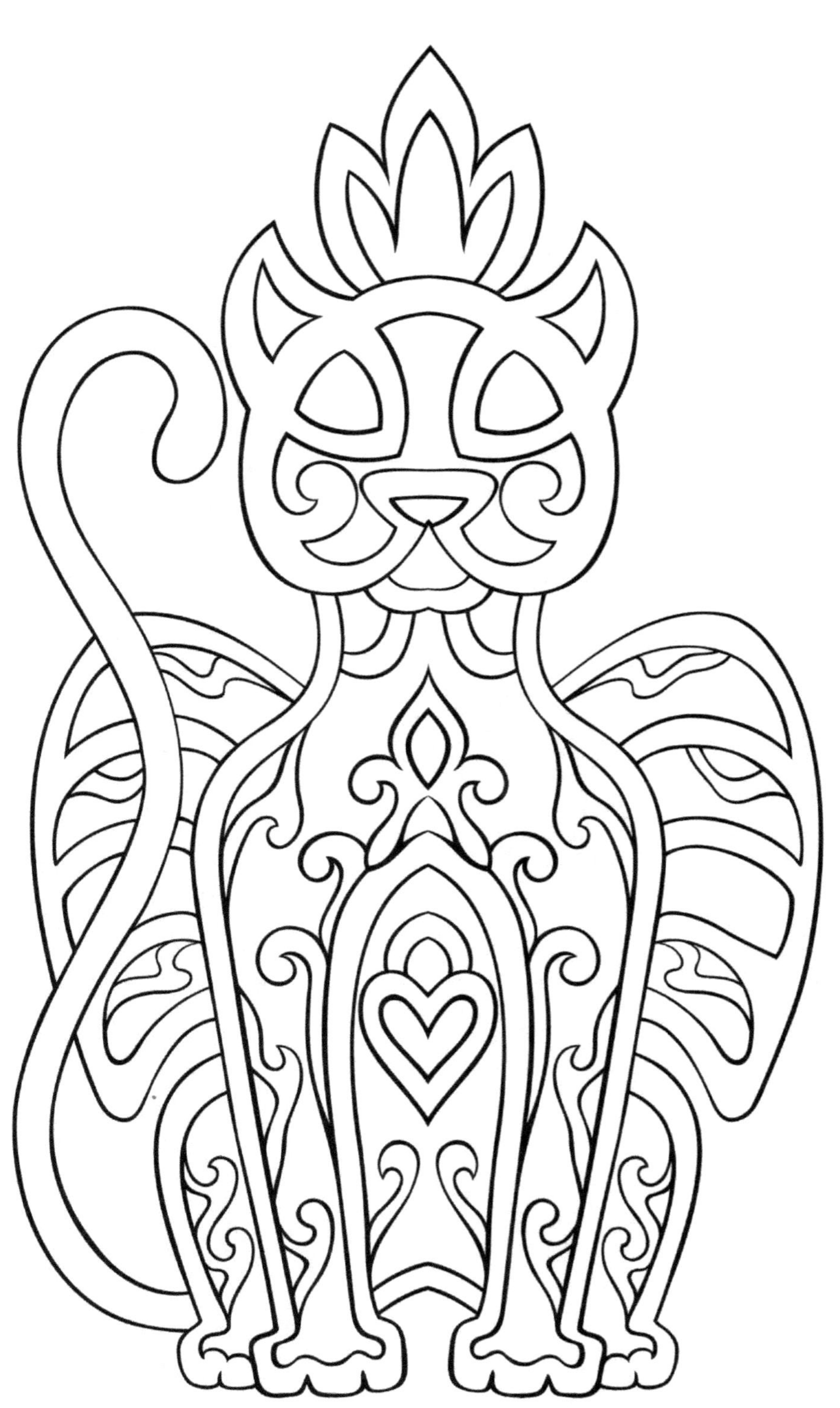

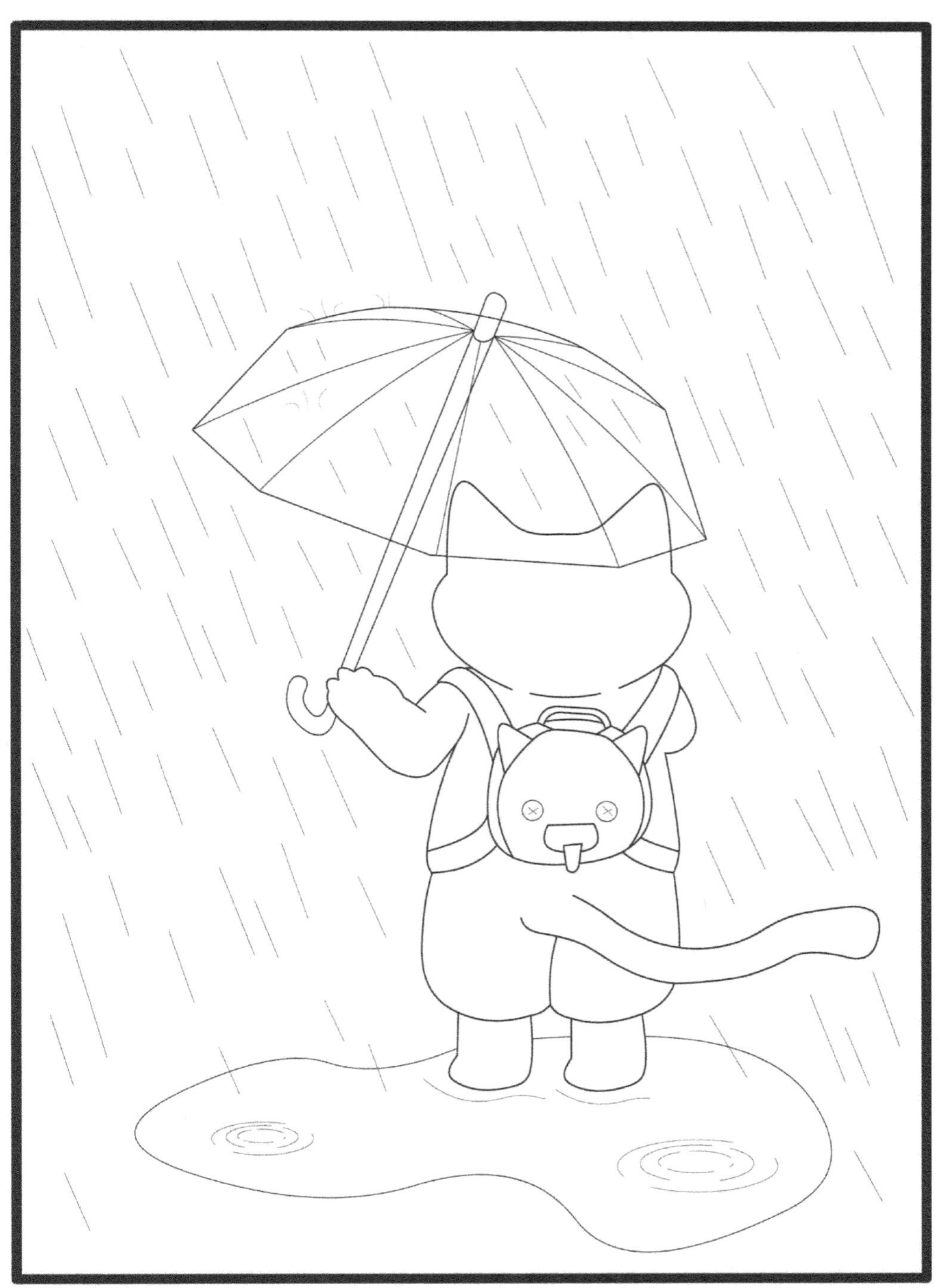

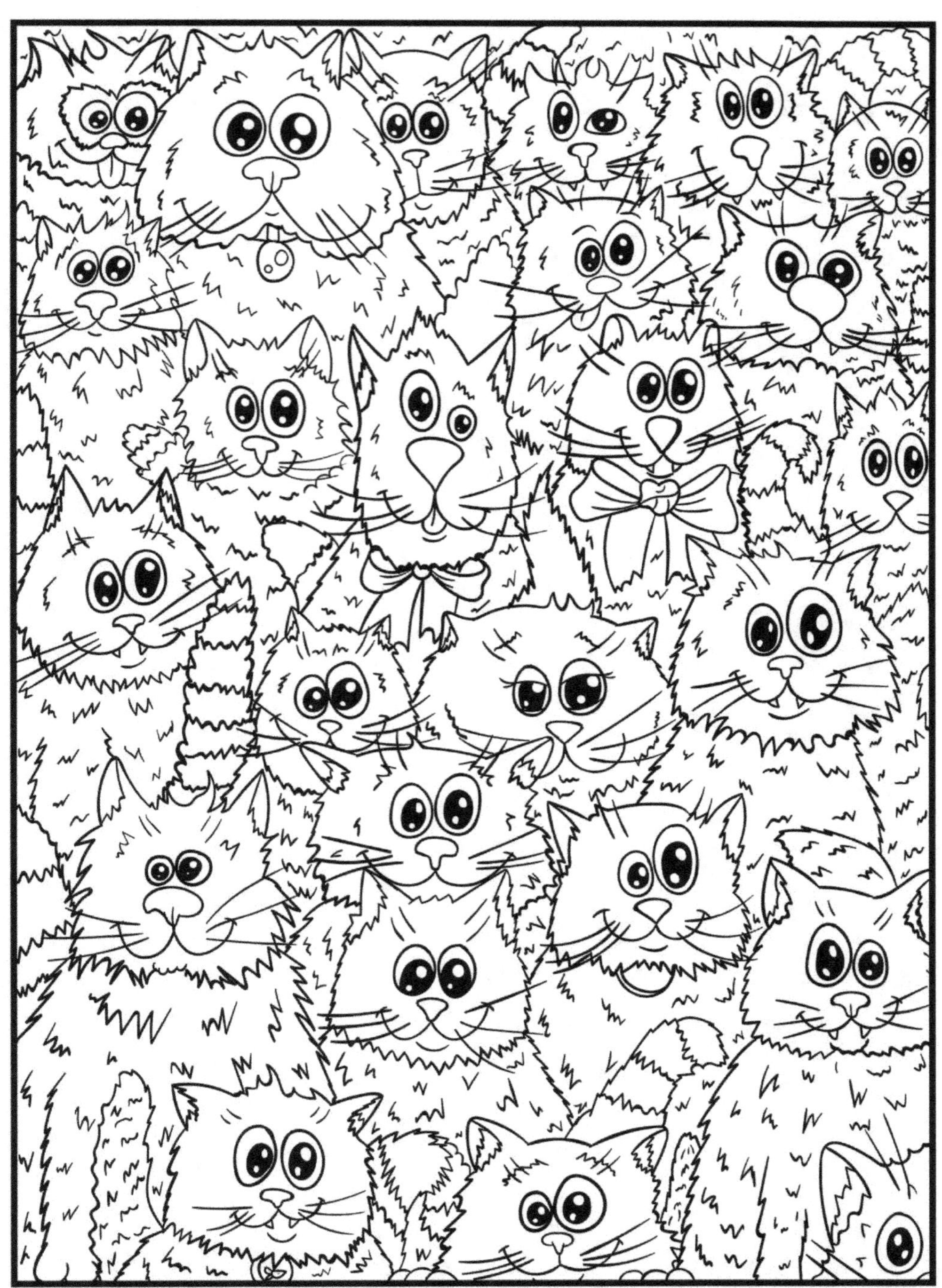

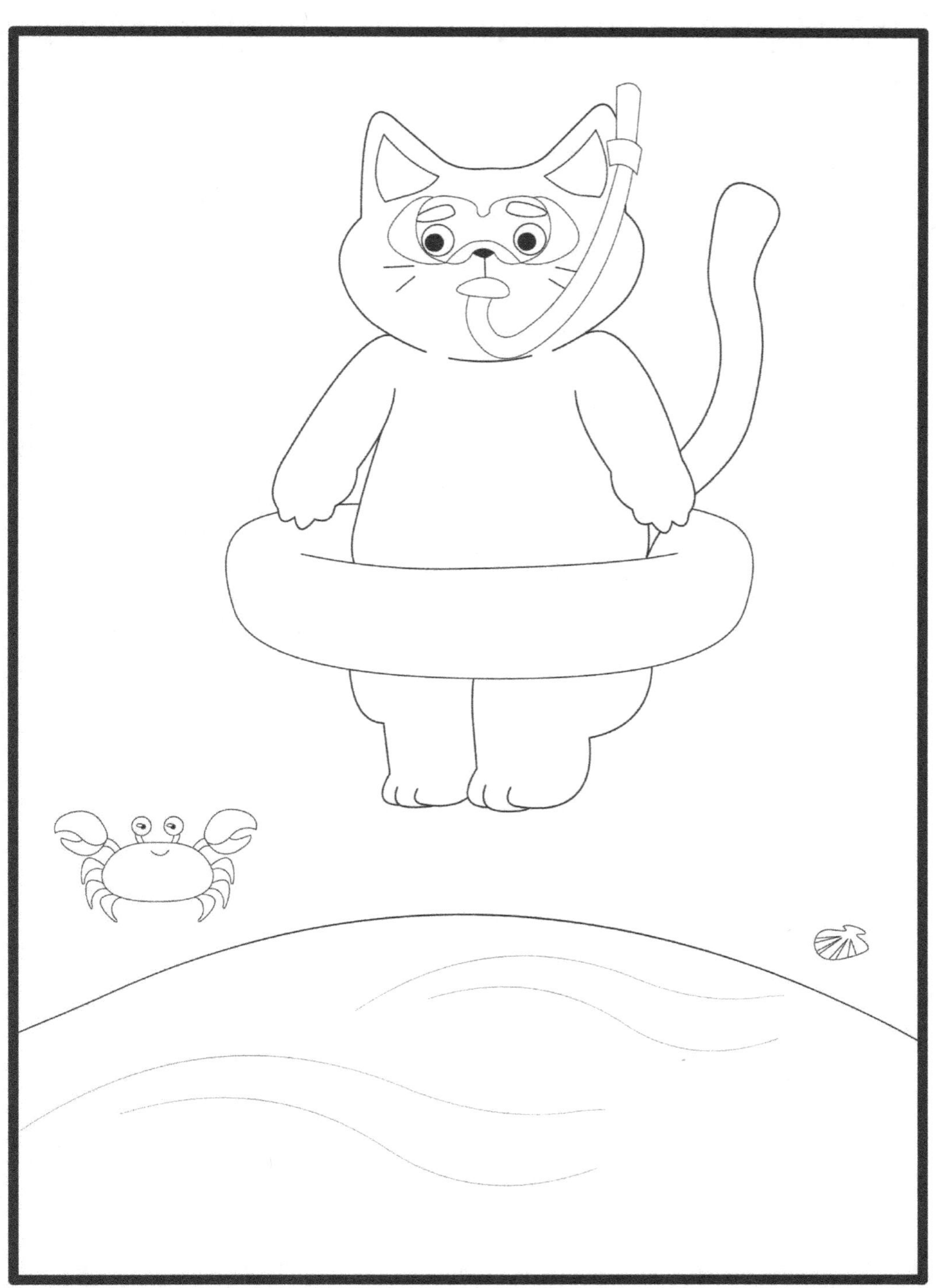

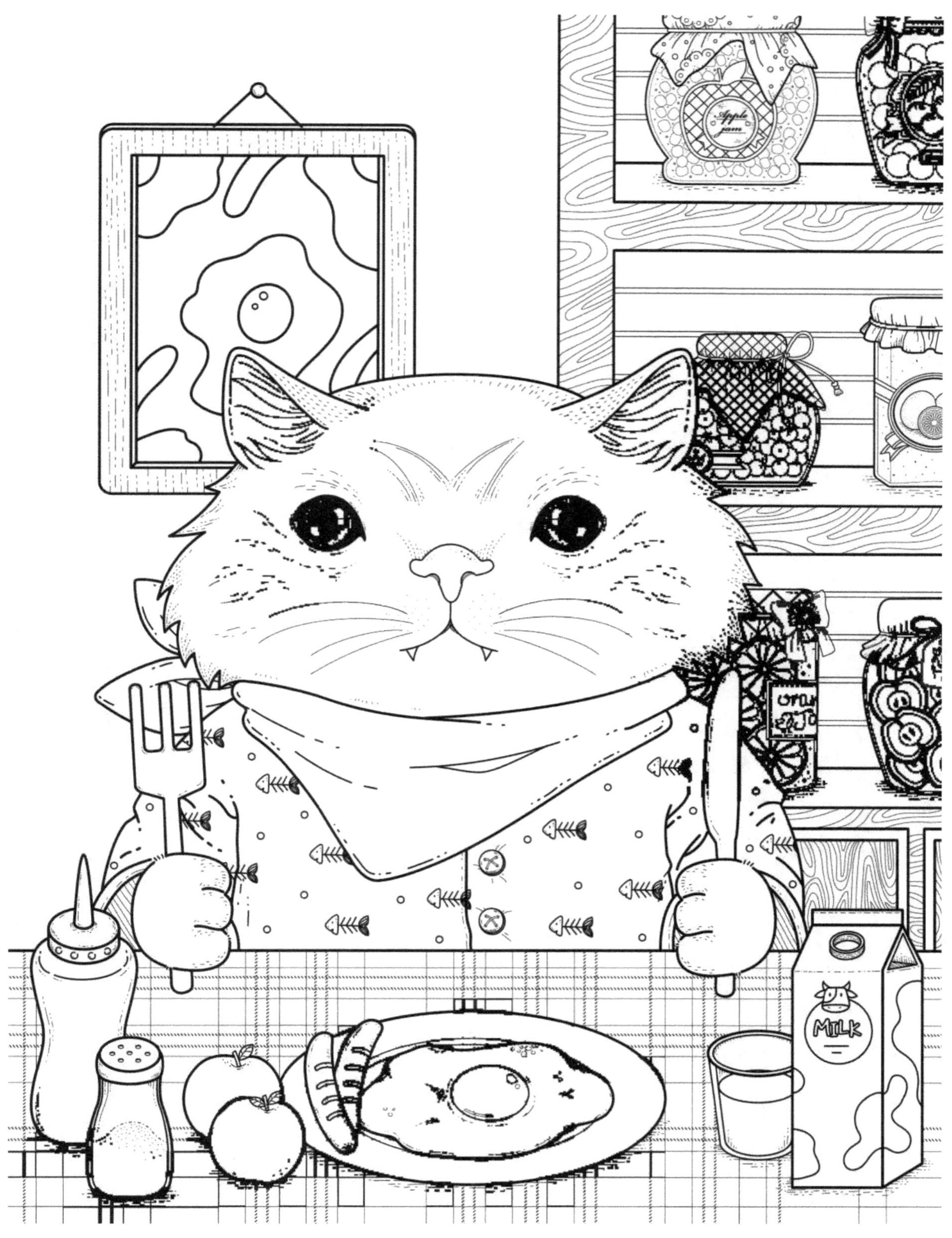
Apple jam
MILK

Thank you for coloring our Cozy Cats Family Coloring Book!

For other great books, check out the Cozy Cat Press website at: www.cozycatpress.com

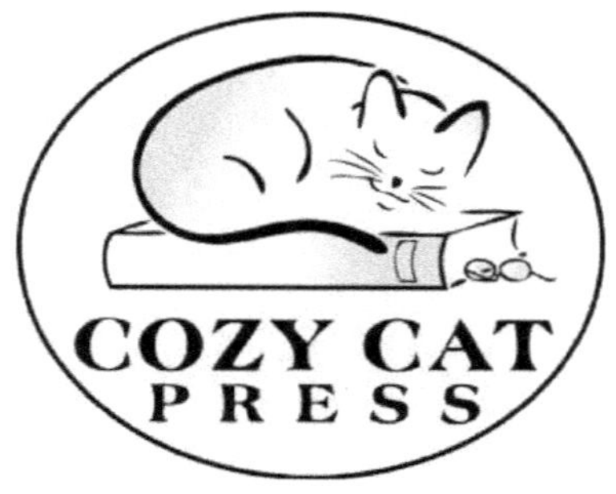

ANNOUNCEMENT:

We would love for you to color our mascot Cozette too! What color is her fur? The book she sleeps on? Her glasses? Send us your own colorful hand-drawn versions of Cozette to cozycatpress@gmail.com. We just may post them on our website!

www.ingramcontent.com/pod-product-compliance
Lightning Source LLC
LaVergne TN
LVHW080328110826
845155LV00026B/223

* 9 7 8 1 9 5 2 5 7 9 0 3 5 *